ALEXANDER ADVENTURES

"OWN THE SCRAWNY"

WRITTEN BY
RICH SAMUELS

This book is a work of fiction. Names, characters, places, and incidents are the product of the author's imagination or are used fictitiously. Any resemblance to actual events, locales, or persons, living or dead, is entirely coincidental.

Copyright © 2014 by Rich Samuels

All Rights Reserved

Cover Design by Sam Rapp

ISBN 978-0-9891880-3-6

Library of Congress Control Number: 2014920587

info@RichPerceptions.com

Explore RichPerceptions.com

No portion of this book may be reproduced in any form without written permission from the publisher or author, except as permitted by U.S. copyright law.

For Lynette

Contents

1. One Million — 1
2. You're an Original — 9
3. That's Not a Good Idea — 17
4. You Can't Handle Stuff Like That — 27
5. The Children's Menu — 31
6. Omelets — 41
7. Make the Most of What You've Got — 47
8. Boots — 53
9. Those are Interesting — 59
10. A Complete Encyclopedia of Lions — 65
11. I Don't Have Big Feet — 69
12. You Should Go Now — 73
13. Scrawny — 79
14. Everything Good? — 83
15. Slimy and Smelly — 89

16.	They Look Up to You	99
17.	The Darrell Question	105
18.	You Guys are Exactly the Same	113
19.	The Prisoner	117
20.	Alexander's Pride	123

Chapter One

One Million

One million views.

One million seven hundred and forty-three views, to be exact.

The video was even turning up in other videos, with titles like *The Top Ten Funniest Viral Videos of the Week*, and even worse, *Biggest Kid Fails of the Month*.

Alexander hadn't looked at it since someone posted it nearly four weeks ago. He had hoped it would just go away, and everyone would forget about it.

They didn't.

One million seven hundred and forty-four views.

He'd tried hard to smile through all the unwanted attention and random staring. After all, it wasn't like he could take back what he did.

One million seven hundred and forty-five views.

The numbers kept climbing.

He clicked on the play button, and the video began.

At first, the image was blurry and chaotic as the camera pushed through the crowd that had gathered in front of the school. Then, in the middle of it all, there he was, facing Melvin—inches away from him, in fact. Melvin was big and muscled, but he was the exact opposite.

Alexander remembered exactly what he was thinking at the time.

Do you really think you can push me around?
Do you think I'm weak, just because I'm small?
Bullies are cowards, and you're no different!

He had believed it, too.

He kept watching the video.

He began to move around Melvin—defensive moves, he thought. Alexander circled around him, making sure that Melvin couldn't get in a punch. He ducked and darted. He didn't stop for an instant. At the time, he felt like a prizefighter.

In the video, he didn't look like a prizefighter at all. For one thing, his shirt was weirdly tucked into the front of his pants, and out everywhere else. Worse, part of the red shirt was peeking through the half-open fly on his pants. He looked odd—but looks weren't his only problem.

While Melvin stood nearly still, Alexander, hunched down and arms raised, danced around him like a crazed monkey. Whoever had created the video even added the sound of a squealing monkey.

The video faded to black, and two words dissolved onto the screen: *Commando Monkey.*

Kids had already been calling him Commando; word had gotten around that he wasn't wearing underwear (at the time, it seemed an obvious defense against wedgies). It was an easy jump for the kid who posted the video—he still didn't know who—to create his new nickname.

And it stuck.

Alexander had been convinced that he was a hero. He was standing up for bullied kids everywhere. He was making a stand and putting bullies in their place. For a minute or two, before Melvin and pretty much everyone else told him that he had it backward and he was the bully, he'd even felt proud of himself.

After that—and especially after the Commando Monkey video was posted online—everyone treated him differently.

Random kids stared and whispered. Other kids followed him, camera phones out and ready to record Commando's Monkey's next viral video.

"You're still looking at that thing?"

At the sound of Anthony's voice, Alexander abruptly clicked off the screen and got up from the curb. He was usually first out of school, but he didn't normally trance out while waiting for his friends. He hadn't heard them walk up, and he didn't know if they had said anything, but they were all staring at him like he'd done something funny. Anthony, Darrell, and Vladimir were there—and Edgar.

Before the *Commando Monkey* video went viral, Alexander barely knew Edgar existed, but now the kid would not stop following him around, laughing at all of his jokes and being borderline creepy. He'd been showing up for weeks at their table at the morning break and at lunch, but never after school—until now. With his big bug eyes and impossibly wide monster smile, he stood by everyone else, like a Commando Monkey fanboy.

But what was he doing here now?

Two or three times a week, Alexander and his friends took an after-school trip to the little snack bar at the car wash, where they shared a pile of the best fries anywhere and watched cars pass through. Alexander viewed the cafe as their private tradition. He'd never thought of bringing anyone else along, yet Edgar looked ready to go.

Sure enough, when they crossed the street in front of the school, Edgar followed like an eager puppy. Despite Alexander's anxiety about what his friends might think, no one said a word.

Then Edgar started talking.

"After school, I go home, but I decided, *Oh, well, why not just go and see what Alexander and his friends are doing?* So I hope you don't mind." He didn't pause for an opinion. He looked up at Vladimir. "Do you have back problems? I heard really tall people have back problems. My uncle had back problems, but he's not as tall as you."

Vladimir opened his mouth to answer, but Edgar was already turning to Anthony. Was he even taking a breath?

"You're a little chubby," he told Anthony, pointing at his stomach. "If you're not careful, you might end up fat. I'm serious."

Edgar was definitely trying way too hard to be liked.

It was embarrassing.

Anthony looked like he had some funny comeback, but Edgar wouldn't let him get a word in, either. He was already watching Darrell's wheelchair rolling along, leading the way.

"How come you're in the wheelchair?"

Darrell stopped abruptly but didn't turn around.

Everyone froze.

"Edgar!" Alexander wished the fanboy would just stop talking.

Darrell turned around, calmly told Edgar, "I was in an accident," and then continued down the sidewalk.

Alexander didn't even have a chance to breathe a sigh of relief before clueless Edgar asked, "How?"

"He doesn't like to talk about it," Alexander explained quickly. *Stop embarrassing me!*

Edgar shrugged and continued walking as if he was totally unaware that he'd said anything wrong.

Darrell, for his part, acted like it was no big deal—but Alexander knew otherwise. He'd undoubtedly blame Alexander for Edgar being there.

Alexander tried to change the subject before things could get worse, asking Darrell, "How's your brother's swimming going? Is he competing?"

It was a completely random question, and Darrell looked over his shoulder with a half-scowl that clearly asked, *Are you crazy?*

When they reached the Car Wash Café, Davina, the craggy old woman who ran the place, looked up from her post behind the counter.

"Boys!"

"Woman!" everyone—except Edgar—answered together. After a moment, Edgar caught on to their long-standing tradition and offered his own solitary, "Woman!"

They didn't have to place an order, of course. Davina put the fries on right away as the boys sat down at their usual table (there were two; theirs was the one closest to the big window overlooking the car wash). Edgar pulled over a chair from the other table, then walked up to the counter and waited patiently until Davina noticed him.

"Eh?" Davina seemed puzzled and suspicious. She didn't know this kid.

Alexander felt uneasy again.

Edgar gazed at a basket of fruit on the counter. "I was wondering if I could have an apple."

An *apple?*

Alexander rushed up to the counter, explaining to Edgar, "We order fries. It's what we do." He pointed at the table. "Then we share."

Edgar looked a bit confused.

"Really?" Darrell laughed at Alexander.

"But fries are unhealthy," Edgar pointed out.

Alexander looked from the fruit basket to the fryer, hoping desperately that Edgar would understand that fries were the right choice.

Darrell rolled his eyes. "Order your apple."

"You should just have fries," Alexander said. "It's what we do."

"Order what you want," Darrell insisted, announcing to everyone, "it's not like we're eight years old with secret club rules."

"I didn't say that." Why was Darrell was mad at him?

"You *act* it."

"I don't," Alexander insisted.

Davina, who had been flipping the fries, turned back to the counter and held out the basket to Edgar. "Apple?"

Edgar nodded and took the apple without hesitation. He walked back to the table and sat down. Alexander was the only one left standing.

Edgar was there because of him—because of *Commando Monkey*. Alexander was just trying to help him fit in.

Darrell, though, didn't seem to understand. He shook his head at Alexander like he'd done something every bit as foolish as the Commando Monkey dance.

Chapter Two

You're an Original

The next morning, during the fifteen-minute "nutrition" break, Alexander stepped into the school library. The hall outside roared with kids rushing to get the most out of their time, but inside there was only peace and quiet.

Mr. Lee, the librarian, looked up from his computer, peered over his glasses, and acknowledged Alexander with a curt nod. He straightened his tie—embroidered with little books dancing across a starry sky—and adjusted his crisp white shirt. After stroking his goatee, he returned to his work.

At the table closest to Mr. Lee's counter, Library Boy sat at his usual place. Before Commando Monkey came along, *that* had been the most well-known nickname in school. *Library Boy* was the one everyone stared at. Even Alexander and his friends had peered in at one time or another. Before, during, and even after school, the gaunt, pasty-faced boy with the oddly long fingers hunched over the same table, surrounded by piles of books and notebooks. He always wore the same thing, too: black jeans and a black, long-sleeved turtleneck shirt, even though it was never that cold. He kept to himself, and rarely looked up. When he did, he never made eye contact.

There were all kinds of crazy rumors about him, but no one really knew why he stayed in the library all the time. Was he diseased? Disturbed? Foreign? No one asked; more rumors flew. Despite how well everyone knew his nickname, though, Library Boy probably had no idea. No one but Mr. Lee talked to him. He was even allowed to eat lunch in the library.

Alexander realized he was staring again, and quickly shifted his attention toward the far end of the library, where sunlight poured through the tall windows. He moved in that direction, straight toward the fiction section, and then to the science fiction area.

He was looking for Ray Bradbury's anthology, *Illustrated Man*, because Vladimir had said there was a story in the book that he might find "interesting," but wouldn't tell him exactly why.

There were two copies on the shelf. As he took one for himself, he thought he saw something move out of the corner of his eye.

He turned, but the aisle was empty. He stood completely still.

He heard breathing nearby.

He walked up close to the shelf, and slowly pulled four books down to create an opening.

A pair of wide eyes stared back at him. The boy looked like a sixth-grader. He was holding up his phone, ready to take a picture or video, but froze in surprise.

Alexander quickly replaced the books, blocking off the kid entirely.

He took *Illustrated Man* to the counter and handed it to Mr. Lee, who smiled politely.

"Alexander!"

"Hi, Mr. Lee."

Mr. Lee looked over the book and nodded in approval. "Classic."

"I guess."

Mr. Lee scanned the book. "I understand you've achieved a touch of fame lately."

Alexander smiled weakly.

"Commando Monkey," Library Boy offered Mr. Lee in a thin, shaky voice. He kept his head bowed and didn't look in Alexander's direction at all.

Mr. Lee nodded in recognition and handed over the book with a smile. "Yes! Commando Monkey."

If Mr. Lee and Library Boy know, is there anyone left who doesn't?

He thanked Mr. Lee and left the library.

The moment he rejoined his friends at their table, Edgar trotted up, more excited than usual.

"Did you see?" Edgar asked him eagerly, then immediately shared with everyone, "*Commando Monkey* hit two million views!"

Alexander caught Darrell shaking his head again.

Edgar was nearly shaking with excitement. "That's, like, cities full of people!"

"Alexander City," Anthony added happily.

"Do people recognize you?" Edgar asked. "Like, on the street?"

"No." Alexander lied. He had, in fact, been recognized three times so far—twice at the mall and once at the movies—by kids he didn't know. Having strange people point and shout "Commando Monkey" was really disturbing.

School, too, was a lost cause. Once, he could slip through crowds nearly undetected, but those days were gone. Not only did everyone know who he was, way too many talked to him.

Ellen and her friends came by the table for their regular visit. Ever since the *Commando Monkey* video, she and her band of darkly clad, vampirish friends made his table a regular stop on their aimless wandering around the lunchroom. Her four friends would cluster behind her as she said hi, and he said hi back. Then she'd ask how he was doing, and he'd say okay, and Ellen and her friends would move on.

Even *that* was changing. This time, they actually sat down at the table, taking every remaining seat.

Ellen nudged Anthony until he moved over. She sat next to Alexander, while Michael, her tall, thin second-in-command, sat on his other side.

"We heard something." Ellen was dead serious.

Michael leaned over menacingly. "And we didn't like what we heard."

Alexander was almost sure he hadn't said anything wrong.

Had he?

"We heard you've been telling people that we're Goths," Michael continued.

And?

Alexander looked at Ellen for a hint. She only glared back.

Michael swatted Alexander on the back. He turned, expecting the worst, but Michael had broken out in a grin. "We're not Goths!"

The Goths—or whatever they were—were suddenly all smiles.

Alexander forced himself to smile too, but he was still totally confused.

"Just because we wear dark clothes doesn't make us Goths," Ellen quietly explained.

Alexander kept smiling. "Well—what are you?"

They were silent again. Alexander really couldn't understand why so many people felt like they had to stare at him.

"What are you?" he asked again, feeling awkward and clueless.

"Do you really want to know?" Ellen whispered.

She paused.

He nodded, suddenly afraid of the answer.

"We're the Art Club," she said.

"Artists," Michael clarified.

"Oh." Alexander wasn't sure what else he could say. It didn't explain a thing.

"But we forgive you," Ellen told him. "We like you."

"You're an original," Michael added.

Alexander didn't want to tell them they were making a mistake. He speculated they were just getting original confused with weird.

Or maybe they weren't confused.

What if this was some artsy way of making fun of him?

Thankfully, Edgar interrupted the silence. Unfortunately, he took the opportunity to share with the artists the news about two million viewers.

"Edgar!" Alexander complained, even though it was already too late.

But Ellen wasn't surprised, repeating, "You're an original."

"Oh!" Edgar nearly knocked over Anthony's drink waving for attention. "You know what we should do? We should have a party! For two million views!"

Alexander wasn't impressed at all. "No."

"Please!"

"Not a good idea," Darrell agreed. Alexander was relieved for his friend's support at first, until Darrell added, "He gets over-excited."

Alexander noticed a kid staring at him from the next table. "Look somewhere else!" he snapped, causing everyone to laugh.

The kid jumped at the rebuke and looked away.

"You should be nicer to your fans," Darrell said calmly as if to annoy Alexander even more.

"I don't have fans. I have stalkers." Alexander thought especially of the boy he'd found behind the shelves in the library.

"And trolls," Edgar added.

"I don't know why you're so mad," Darrell teased. "You're famous."

"Trolls?" Alexander asked Edgar. It was an odd thing to say.

Edgar nodded. "On the comments! You have so many trolls."

Alexander felt for his phone in his pocket. He hadn't thought about the comments. He'd only looked at the video.

Anthony gave Edgar a dismissive wave as if the whole thing was a joke, telling Alexander, "Don't look at the comments."

Alexander was instantly worried. "What's in the comments?" he asked Edgar.

Edgar was excited to help. "You know, people are just crazy online!"

"What do they say?"

"Nothing," Anthony interrupted. "Don't read that stuff."

"Don't read them," Darrell insisted, which convinced Alexander he'd better do the opposite.

The bell rang. Usually, they all walked to P.E. together, but Alexander used the indisputable restroom excuse and went in the opposite direction. He started to circle around the back of one of the school buildings—it would give him just enough uninterrupted time to check.

He took out his smartphone and called up the video.

Four thousand three hundred and twenty-four comments.

The huge number seemed insane. Why would so many people have an opinion?

He slowed and then stopped walking as he began to scroll down and read the comments.

Is there something wrong with him?

Trolls, Edgar had said. He tried to keep that in mind. He couldn't let crazy comments bother him.

What is he, six?

He already knew he'd been acting immature. He figured that was a fair comment.

If he did that to me, I'd punch him.

He didn't expect a violent comment and thought about stopping right there. He even put his phone back in his pocket but pulled it right out again.

He had to keep reading.

What a baby.

Scrawny, isn't he?

Scrawny?

He was small, but *scrawny?*

Then, there were those who couldn't be bothered with anything more than one-word comments.

Loser.

Mutant.

Moron.

And then *that* word again:

Scrawny.

Alexander vaguely heard the bell ring. He was standing alone in the middle of the grass courtyard. He couldn't stop reading.

Odd.

Idiot.

Definitely a monkey.

It was horrible that people were making fun of him, but they were *hating*, too.

Hating!

And worse:

Fake. Nobody would really act like that.

Some people didn't even believe he was real.

Chapter Three

That's Not a Good Idea

Alexander was so late to P.E., he was the very last person out of the locker room. He ran out to the field and tried to quietly take his place in line with his squad, but Coach Strathers noticed him and abruptly stopped calling roll.

Alexander heard the snickering all around him, but ignored everyone and looked straight ahead as if he hadn't done anything wrong.

The coach thought differently, though, pointing at him and then at the field—Strathers Sign Language for *YOU! RUN A LAP!*

Alexander took off and started running. He didn't mind the punishment—running was actually the only thing he liked about P.E. He could run a mile a lot easier than some kids who nearly got sick trying. Maybe one day, if he ever grew longer legs, he'd actually be good at it.

When he finished his run and sat back down with his squad, his stomach nearly flipped anyway.

Coach Strathers stood in front of the class with two objects in his hands:

A baseball bat and a softball.

Alexander had learned to accept basketball, where he was at an obvious height disadvantage. He'd learned how to run with the pack in soccer. He'd even come to tolerate handball in small doses.

Softball was an entirely different story.

Supposedly, a softball was softer than a regular baseball, but Alexander didn't think by much. The softball bats were still bats—*they* weren't soft—and he'd seen them slide out of a person's hands like missiles.

They could easily hit somebody.

In softball, it wasn't possible to run with the pack, like it was in soccer, basketball, or touch football. He would be assigned a position in the field, and if the ball came to him, it was his and his only, to be caught, missed, or, if he was at-bat, to actually hit. Being at-bat also meant that he would be in the direct path of the not-very-soft softball. If he was lucky, maybe he'd hit the ball with the bat, but if he wasn't, the ball would hit him right in the face.

The last time he'd been forced to play softball, in sixth grade, he'd done his research and discovered that the safest place—the quietest place—was right field. Most kids didn't hit in that direction, and even the occasional lefty wasn't likely to hit a ball that far out. He'd successfully convinced his team captain that he wasn't very skilled (honesty never hurt) and for the good of the team, he should be out in right field. He was relieved and happy to take his position. He figured he'd achieved his goal and could relax.

As soon as he was out there, though, his mind had begun to wander. He watched the clouds in the sky above home plate, and the trees over the fence. Eventually, he noticed a discarded golf tee at his feet. That seemed odd, so he picked it up for closer inspection. At that very moment, someone screamed his name. He looked toward the infield, figuring a ball was headed his way. He didn't see anything and felt relieved.

They still screamed, though—but not because a ball was heading his way.

It was already there, resting in the grass by his left foot.

Alexander scooped up the ball in a panic and threw it somewhere toward the infield.

It was too late. By the time the ball had reached the catcher at home base, the opposing team had scored twice.

For months, kids accused him of picking daisies in the outfield.

These days, he knew better. He had no intention of making that mistake again. If he forced himself to pay attention, right field would still be a good option.

"Hey!"

Vladimir was standing right next to him, gently nudging him with his right foot.

"Get up!"

Alexander blinked and realized he was sitting alone. Everyone else was already heading out to the field. He got to his feet.

"I was only *thinking*," he told Vladimir, anticipating the obvious question.

They followed the rest of their squadmates out to the most distant softball field. The opposing team—he wasn't surprised to see that it was Melvin's squad—was already huddled together.

Alexander headed straight for Ben, his own team captain, certain that he'd gladly agree to the Right Field Option. Before he had a chance to say anything, though, Ben pointed directly at him and said, "First base."

"That's not a good idea," Alexander said. He looked at the rest of the team. "I'm not very good." He thought he sounded pretty reasonable.

"First base," Ben repeated, just a little louder.

"That's the worst possible idea," Alexander insisted as if it were a scientific fact. He added a little fake laugh for good measure. He looked at Vladimir, who didn't seem like he was going to be any help.

"Just put him in right field," suggested Charlie, a boy Alexander knew vaguely from elementary school. Back then, Charlie had played in a real baseball league. Sometimes he'd even come to school in his uniform. He wasn't huge and tall like Vladimir, but Alexander thought he could easily pass for fifteen.

Alexander pointed at Charlie and began to reason with Ben. "See, he played baseball, and—"

"First base," Ben interrupted, pointed at his own chest with his thumb. "I'm the captain."

Behind Ben, Alexander realized that the other team was watching impatiently from behind the backstop fence.

Alexander kept calm and shook his head. "I'm just not going to play first base. It's a bad idea."

"First base."

Alexander hesitated, considering his next move.

A whistle blew in his ear. He hadn't noticed Coach Strathers, who had walked up right beside him.

"Why is it always you, Alexander?"

Carefully, Alexander stated his case: "I just don't think it's a good idea for me to play first base."

Coach nodded as if he were seriously considering Alexander's words. "And that's where your team captain wants you to play?"

"Yeah," Alexander answered, hoping he was sounding adequately mystified.

Coach nodded again. "I see your point."

Alexander smiled with satisfaction as Ben's eyes widened in growing outrage.

"Okay," Coach said, patting him briskly on the shoulder. "You're the pitcher."

In unison, Alexander and Ben responded with a desperate, "No!"

"He doesn't know *how* to pitch," Charlie added.

"Then teach him, champ."

"Can't I put him somewhere else? Anywhere?" Ben asked, looking over Alexander like he was the worst athlete in the world. "He's *scrawny*."

Scrawny?

Coach smiled. "You can't handle your team." He looked over at Alexander. "And you're not happy with your position. Problem solved."

Scrawny!

Coach walked away, leaving all eyes on Alexander. He avoided everyone's gaze. He knew what he'd see in their eyes. Now he knew exactly what they were thinking.

Scrawny, isn't he?

"Have you ever pitched?" Charlie asked.

"I've pitched," Alexander answered. He'd thrown a ball—which he figured was the same thing, technically.

Charlie didn't look convinced.

The squad converged on the bag of gloves laying against the backstop, while the other team still waited for them to get their act together.

Alexander reached in and removed a mitt. He tried it on, punching the palm of his hand like a baseball player. It seemed unusually large and stiff.

Charlie walked up to him and yanked the mitt off of his hand. "That's a catcher's mitt," he said. He reached into the bag, pulled out another glove, and shoved it at Alexander's chest. "*This* is a pitcher's glove."

Moron.

Alexander reluctantly took the glove, which was much more flexible, and walked out to the pitcher's mound. When he turned back to the plate, Charlie was already in position as catcher. He threw the ball to Alexander, but it sailed over his head into the still-unoccupied outfield. He turned back to Charlie, who looked back at him like he was insane.

"Get the ball!" Charlie barked.

Alexander ran and got the ball. Charlie was obviously a little touchy, though Alexander thought he was being unfair. After all, *he* was the one who threw the ball too high.

When Alexander got back to the pitcher's mound, Vladimir had taken up his position just over his right shoulder, and the other players were already in the outfield.

"Hey, *short*stop," Alexander called to Vladimir. He knew it was a stupid joke, but Vladimir just waved with his glove hand, failing to see the irony or the humor in being the tallest kid in school playing shortstop.

"Pitch," Charlie said flatly.

Alexander threw the ball toward Charlie, but it veered off to the right and hit the backstop fence.

Ben threw his mitt down on first base. "Come on, Alexander!"

Charlie stared at Alexander for a moment, then advised him, in a much calmer voice, "It's *softball*, Alexander—you don't throw overhand." He recovered the ball and tossed it back. "And take it easy."

Alexander nodded at Charlie and tried again, underhand this time and more gently. He was hoping for a few more practice pitches, but the opposing team sent out their first batter.

In front of Charlie, just beside home plate, Melvin stood with bat in hand.

Alexander broke out in a cold sweat.

For a few minutes, he'd forgotten that there was a batter involved, whose sole purpose was to hit the ball as hard as he could in Alexander's direction.

He looked at Charlie's ornate catcher's mask and thought that it would make much more sense for a pitcher to have that kind of protection. A softball could easily break his nose or knock out some teeth. He could get a black eye or a concussion. Maybe the ball would come in lower—he couldn't even begin to imagine how badly *that* might turn out. With Melvin at-bat, anything could happen.

"Pitch the ball already," Ben told him.

Alexander took a deep breath. He would have to react quickly to avoid catastrophe.

Melvin stood rock solid. His face was expressionless. He waited for Alexander to pitch.

Alexander threw the ball into his own glove, casually eyeing first base and then third base. He'd seen baseball games—that's what pitchers did.

"There's nobody on base yet, Alexander," Ben reminded him, with a weariness that Alexander thought translated directly to *idiot*.

He pitched the ball and immediately crouched down to make himself a smaller target. He covered his head with his arms, just in case.

He didn't see the outcome of the pitch, but someone yelled, "Strike!"

Alexander dared to peek through his arms.

Ben threw his glove down again. "Stand up, Alexander!"

Melvin shook his head in disbelief, as if he were posting a comment on the video.

What is he, six?

Charlie, still crouched in his catcher's stance, glared at him too, probably wondering, Is there something wrong with him?

Vladimir stared at his glove, avoiding eye contact.

Alexander stood up and brushed off his shorts as casually as he could, though they weren't dirty. Then he carefully pitched the ball again.

This time, he forced himself not to duck when Melvin hit the ball, but he couldn't help but flinch a little when it sailed a foot over his head. It hit the ground just beyond midfield, and by the time the center fielder scooped it up and threw it to second base, Melvin was already safe.

Still, Alexander felt a bit proud of himself for standing tall in spite of the speeding softball. He shrugged at Ben as if to say, *We can't win them all*, but Ben didn't seem to like his attitude at all. He stormed right up to Alexander from first base, his face red with anger. Alexander was so surprised that he held up his glove in front of his chest as sort of instinctive protection.

"Catch the ball when it comes to you!" Ben shouted in his face. Then he turned and stomped right back to first base. Alexander stood awkwardly atop the pitcher's mound, waiting desperately for the next batter, and trying to forget that everyone on both teams were probably thinking the same thing:

Is there something wrong with him?

Charlie watched it all from behind home plate, his arms crossed in a way that Alexander thought wasn't very supportive.

He threw a slow, easy pitch to the next batter, making sure to stick his glove up just above his head, so Ben would see that he was ready. The ball popped up, though, and fell right into the mitt of the third baseman. The batter was out—but Melvin was still at second base. Alexander could feel his stare searing the back of his neck.

The next player at bat was another familiar face: Edgar. He gave Alexander a quick (and embarrassing) little wave, and then proceeded to strike out. Alexander decided that maybe he'd better rethink the fanboy thing.

The next batter actually got a hit, but luckily it was just a ground ball. Vladimir snagged it, fired it to Ben, and forced the batter out.

Stepping off the mound, Alexander felt like he could breathe again.

He wasn't disappointed (or surprised) that he struck out in his single turn at bat, but was just short of shocked when Charlie walked up to take his place next to home plate, nodded, and said, "Good try."

Right away, Alexander felt badly. It hadn't, in fact, been a good try at all. He didn't expect Charlie to be friendly, yet he talked to Alexander like he was a teammate. It was confusing.

At bat, Charlie hit the ball so far that it landed in the next field over. Alexander wasn't surprised in the least.

By the time Coach blew his whistle, sending them back to the locker room, they'd barely finished an inning.

He'd survived—but there were countless weeks to go.

Alexander started back across the field, walking alongside Vladimir.

At first, Vladimir didn't say anything. Then he laughed, shook his head and teased, "Pitcher?"

"Be quiet."

Chapter Four

You Can't Handle Stuff Like That

As Alexander entered the outdoor cafeteria area and moved through the sea of tables, he tried not to look anyone in the eye, but he knew they were staring. Did they all think he was a *moron*, or a *loser*, or *scrawny?*

He knew he had to be extra careful when he approached the table he shared with his friends. He carefully lifted his feet over the bench and sat down as normally as he possibly could, afraid that one wrong move would draw even more attention.

He didn't dare smile.

"I *told* you not to read the comments," Darrell said.

"I couldn't help it."

Anthony tried to be helpful. "Don't believe that stuff."

"I don't." Even to Alexander, that sounded lame.

Darrell smiled. "You can't handle stuff like that."

"They're just trolls," Anthony assured him.

"I can handle anything you can, Darrell," Alexander snapped. He turned to Anthony next. "And I know they're trolls. I'm not stupid."

"I know that," Anthony insisted, and Alexander knew instantly he'd overreacted.

Again.

"See?" Darrell threw up his hands as if to say, *There's your proof!*"

"Just forget about it," Anthony said.

Alexander *wanted* to forget about it, but he couldn't help wondering if his friends were thinking what everyone online seemed to think: *Is there something wrong with him?*

What would happen if he actually looked through all four thousand three hundred and twenty-four (probably more now) comments? Eight hundred and twenty-three might call him scrawny. A thousand might say he was just weird. Two thousand might want to *hit* him. Would he even find one person that would be on his side?

"Hey!" Anthony shoved his arm lightly, snapping him out of his near-trance. "Stop thinking about it."

Alexander smiled gamely like he got the message, and was ready to talk about something else.

Edgar finally joined them at the table, though, and eagerly wanted to know, "Did you read them?"

Alexander didn't answer, but his expression gave him away.

Edgar was excited. "You did! Weren't they crazy?"

Alexander hoped one of his friends would tell Edgar to cool it, but no one did. Darrell crunched on his cucumber sandwich and watched with a faint smile.

"There was one guy who said you looked like you needed your diaper changed," Edgar laughed. "People are so harsh."

Ellen and her artist friends sat down at the table without preamble. "It means nothing," she said. "They don't know you."

Embarrassed, Alexander faked another smile. "I know."

Some of the comments might be from people who knew him, though. Maybe it meant *something*.

What was he supposed to do about that?

Edgar was giggling at his phone—likely looking at more *Commando Monkey* comments, Alexander guessed. Though Vladimir was trying not to be obvious, he was reading over Edgar's shoulder.

He realized people all around him were looking at their phones. There was a good chance they were looking at *Commando Monkey*.

On the walk home, just before they got to Alexander's house, Anthony told him again, "Don't let it bother you."

"I'm not." Despite Alexander's best efforts, the anxiety in his voice was obvious.

They reached Alexander's house first.

"Well," Anthony began, as if he'd come to a decision, "I'll see you at six."

"Huh?"

"I'll see you at six," Anthony repeated.

"We don't have—"

"—at six. Sleepover, my house." Anthony sounded like he was reminding Alexander, but Alexander knew they hadn't made any plans at all. Anthony just didn't want him to spend the night looking at thousands of comments.

"At six," Anthony started for his own house, denying Alexander any chance to protest.

Chapter Five

The Children's Menu

At exactly six o'clock, Alexander stood outside Anthony's front door. He took a deep breath, decided to put the comments out of his mind, and pounded as hard as he could. He wasn't trying to be obnoxious—if he knocked politely, no one would hear him for ages.

Right away, the door swung open, and Anthony greeted him with a loud and happy "*Hi!*" clearly announcing his arrival to the entire house. When he was small, Alexander imagined that Anthony was signaling everyone inside to start moving, as if they were actors in a play. The truth was, Anthony's family never stopped moving.

"*Hi!*" he shouted back, just to prove to Anthony that he wouldn't be outdone. He instantly felt better and stepped forward into chaos. Right away, he was nearly run over by Anthony's ten-year-old twin brothers, Charlie and Eric. They were running around the house, holding their tablets practically up to their noses while involved in some sort of multiplayer game. Anthony's four-year-old sister, Ellie, was sprawled out on the floor of the den with their mom, working on some sort of craft project.

Elsewhere in the house, Alexander could hear Anthony's dad hammering away at one of his endless projects. Five cats added to the madness, though they darted across the floor so fast there could have been ten of them if Alexander didn't know better. Anthony's mom saw Alexander and gave him an Anthony-style "*Hi!-*" which Ellie immediately echoed. Somewhere in the house the twins took the cue and shouted back in unison, "Hey, Alexander!" and then almost instantly jumped in front of him.

"Are you coming to our birthday?" Eric asked.

Alexander nodded. "Of course," he said. The twins happily gave each other high fives, which made him feel a lot like a big brother.

Anthony led Alexander into the garage through a door right off the kitchen. His dad stood amidst a scattering of loose wood planks, his hammer hanging from his tool belt as he measured a two-by-four and marked it with a pencil. He looked up at Alexander with a wide smile exactly like Anthony's.

"Hey, Alex!" Anthony's dad, Joe, extended an arm and solidly shook Alexander's hand, looking him straight in the eye and making him feel like he was some sort of important businessman or something.

"Hey, Joe!" Alexander replied. Anthony's dad always insisted on his first name.

"How's it going?"

Alexander nodded his head and pointed at the woodpile. "What are you building?"

"A computer desk. It doesn't look like much now," Joe pulled out a rough sketch, "but it's going to be pretty sweet, don't you think?"

Alexander peered at the drawing and nodded politely, though he really couldn't make sense of the vague jumble.

Scotty, the black cat that Anthony claimed was his own, darted between Alexander's legs and headed outside through the open garage door. According to Anthony, each cat "belonged" to a different family member, but the cats seemed to be out of the loop on that one.

Anthony and his sister Ellie had their own rooms, while Charlie and Eric shared theirs. Anthony's room was so small and narrow there was just barely enough room on the floor for Alexander to sleep. Alexander used Charlie's ratty sleeping bag. It smelled pretty gross, like a combination of dirty socks and rotting leaves, but he never complained. He felt like he was an honorary brother, and brothers didn't care about things like that.

Alexander dropped his backpack onto the bedroom floor and headed to the kitchen with Anthony for some snacks. That plan was foiled, though, when Anthony's mom shouted, all the way from the den, "Out of the kitchen!"

Anthony swiped a couple of cookies anyway and handed one over. Alexander quickly shoved it into his mouth whole to destroy the evidence.

"She's not going to frisk you," Anthony assured him.

Alexander wiped the crumbs from his mouth and chewed as fast as he could, just in case.

Usually, whenever Alexander slept over, Anthony's family went out to dinner. They didn't go anywhere fancy—sometimes it was just a fast food restaurant.

This time, they pulled up outside a creaky-looking restaurant, with a blinking neon sign that advertised the strangely plain name of "Coffee Shop."

It was the kind of ancient, worn place that Alexander's parents would never even *think* of going. Mom would probably call it a *greasy spoon*. Usually, they went to places that included "cafe" or "bistro" in the name and were decorated with hanging brass kitchen utensils and coordinated colors. Coffee Shop had no brass at all and looked just as faded inside as it did outside. Big wooden booths with patched orange vinyl seats dominated the restaurant. All seven of them could fit into one booth with room to spare, making Alexander wonder if people were just bigger in the old days. There were old black and white pictures on the walls of the coffee shop from fifty or sixty years ago. Alexander couldn't help staring. *Why* couldn't they come up with a better name after all that time?

The family moved like a wave toward their booth. Alexander had learned a long time ago that when he was with Anthony's family, he had to move with the tide. If they wanted to go, he was going. It was useless to resist.

He did, however, hold Anthony back until the twins slid into their side of the booth. Alexander made sure he sat on the outside. The idea of being trapped all the way on the inside of a long booth gave him the chills. He liked his freedom.

On the other side of the table, Anthony's mom and dad sat with Ellie between them.

A waitress walked up to the table. She was a wiry woman with rough, deep wrinkles and gray hair in a bun, and she looked as if she'd been there since the place opened. She pressed a stack of menus against her chest.

"My name is Deborah. I'll be your waitress today." She began to hand out the menus—the first to Anthony's mom—and continued, "We have three specials today—"

As Deborah spoke, she placed a kids' menu—a paper placemat covered with cartoons and word-search puzzles—right in front of Alexander.

Suddenly, the specials weren't important.

Anthony, meanwhile, got a normal adult menu.

Alexander picked up a corner of his kids' menu with his fingertips and let it droop as he suspended it in front of Deborah.

"I'd like a regular menu, please." He tried to be polite about it. *All sweetness and light*, as his mom would say.

Deborah raised an eyebrow. Instead of instantly taking back his kids' menu and giving him what he asked for, she looked over at Anthony's mom, who nodded her approval.

"He's older than he looks."

Deborah took back the kids' menu and handed Alexander the regular menu with what he thought was a massively insincere smile. She turned to Anthony's parents. "I'll be right back to take your order."

Alexander watched her walk to another table, staring until Anthony poked him in the side.

When Deborah came back a few minutes later, Alexander made sure he was very clear: "I want the spaghetti and meatballs. With tomato sauce on the side. And the meatballs, too."

Deborah stopped writing. "Sauce on the side?"

"And the meatballs."

She looked at him doubtfully. "And the meatballs?"

"Yes."

"You want the meatballs and spaghetti, but you don't want the meatballs or sauce on the spaghetti, is that right?"

"He's picky," Anthony apologized.

"Yes," Alexander answered, feeling a bit smug. "I like to put it on myself."

At that, the twins broke out in a giggling fit.

Anthony nudged him. "On yourself?"

It took Alexander a second to realize what he'd said. "You know what I mean," he clarified, then added to make sure, "I like to put it on *the spaghetti* myself."

They all laughed anyway.

Except Deborah.

Whatever.

When it came time for the twins to order, both ordered the meatballs and spaghetti with sauce and meatballs on the side, and each made sure to let Deborah know, through gasping laughter, "I like to put it on myself."

Deborah took it all stoically, but Alexander thought she'd given him a dirty look just before she left the table.

The twins were still giggling.

Alexander waited patiently for everyone to calm down. He was resigned to moments like this. It wasn't the first time people laughed at his strategies, and it wouldn't be the last. Now that he knew what people thought of him, though, it felt different.

He wasn't being unreasonable. He hadn't made the special order just to annoy Deborah. He loved spaghetti and meatballs, but it was one of those meals that he thought should have a yellow *caution* flag right in the center. If he didn't handle it just right, he could end up looking like a messy little kid, with sauce splattered all over his shirt. Most restaurants, in his experience, liked to soak the spaghetti in sauce, making it almost impossible to eat safely. Handling spaghetti and meatballs the *right* way separated the men from the boys.

He had worked out the perfect method to eat spaghetti. First, he'd take his knife and cut the spaghetti across several times. Then, he'd take a spoonful of the sauce and apply it evenly across the top of the spaghetti, not mixing it in, but just sprinkling it on the top. He'd eat the meatballs with the spaghetti—but off their own plate, where he could more easily cut them into small, bite-sized chunks. Follow the rules and *no splatter*.

Maybe he'd write an app about it: *How To Eat Neat*.

Anthony poked him again. "My dad said something to you, trance-boy."

"Sorry." Alexander blinked and looked at Joe.

"Congratulations on your million views."

"Two million," Anthony corrected, nudging Alexander at the same time as if it were a big joke.

Alexander answered politely, "It's not my video."

"You are the video," Anthony assured him.

"Can we *please* talk about something else?"

"Commando Monkey!" Charlie said, sending Eric into hysterics. Alexander had once read a story about twin boys who couldn't stand each other, and kept plotting to do each other in—unlike Charlie and Eric, who worked together way too often, in his opinion.

"So, does this place have any real name?" Alexander asked, hoping to change the subject.

Joe looked overly puzzled, then perked up and declared, "Let's ask the manager!" He quickly raised his hand and called out (too loudly, a family trait) to the closest waitress, "Excuse me!"

Alexander couldn't help but sink a little in his seat. Anthony poked him *again*.

A waitress came over and Joe asked to see the manager.

Now Anthony giggled, and told Alexander, "She's going to think there's something wrong!"

Alexander wanted to crawl under the table.

The manager came over to the table, concerned.

"Is everything okay?" she asked.

"Oh, everything's fine," Joe cheerfully assured her. Then he gestured to Alexander. "My young friend here has a question for you."

Alexander tried to wave her away. "It's not that important."

Concerned, the manager insisted, "I'm here, what can I do for you?"

Now he felt obligated.

"It's not a big deal." *Please go away.*

Deborah returned to the table. "Is everything okay?"

The manager gestured to Alexander. "This boy has a question."

"Oh, really?" Deborah asked, another artificial smile plastered across her face.

"What can we help you with?" the manager asked again, squatting down next to him and making him feel small.

"Go for it, ask the question," Anthony's mom encouraged him.

"*Please* do," Deborah said.

No way out.

"Go ahead," Anthony's mom repeated, and he knew he had no choice.

Everyone at the table was looking at him. He felt his heart beating.

Alexander looked directly at the manager, so that Deborah would know he was ignoring her. "I was wondering why this place is just called *Coffee Shop*. How come it doesn't have a real name?"

Deborah crossed her arms, as if she was getting impatient.

The manager, still crouching next to him, placed a menu on the table and pointed at the photo on the cover. "*Well*, fifty-three years ago, when John Callister founded the restaurant, he thought that maybe..."

She spoke slowly and carefully. Like a kindergarten teacher.

Comments about *Commando Monkey* were bad enough. Now he was being trolled in person.

Chapter Six

Omelets

Alexander opened his eyes to blinding sunlight streaming in through Anthony's bedroom window. Anthony stood over him, fully dressed, poking him through the sleeping bag with his toe.

"You really have to stop poking me," Alexander said, blocking the sunlight with his arm, but secretly grateful. He'd been having a nightmare about checking the comments on his smartphone and finding out there were half a million.

The incredible, unmistakable smell of breakfast at Anthony's wafted through the room. While Alexander's parents made a big deal out of dinner, Anthony's parents were all about breakfast. It pushed his dream—his nightmare—far off to the back of his mind.

"Are you going to sleep all morning?" Anthony asked.

Alexander stretched. "What time is it?"

"Ten."

Alexander sat up suddenly in the sleeping bag. He was a morning person, and at ten the day felt like it was half-over. "Why didn't you wake me up?"

"I tried." Anthony looked at Alexander's hand. "Do you always sleep like that?"

Alexander realized he'd been grasping his phone all night, so tightly his fingers ached. He noticed a text from Edgar.

Did you see the *Commando Monkey* parody?

A parody video? If the original wasn't bad enough, now people had *another* way to make fun of him. The idea was horrifying, but he couldn't help but tap on Edgar's link.

Anthony grabbed the phone out of his hands, shoved it into his pocket, and headed for breakfast before Alexander could protest.

The instant he reached the kitchen, Alexander forgot about his phone. Every counter was filled with breakfast food, from cereal to waffles to pancakes, fruit, and bacon. A toaster stood at the ready, with choices of bread and bagels. There was orange juice, of course, but also grapefruit juice. The twins were checking things out; Ellie was already seated and waiting to be served. Anthony's mom retrieved milk from the refrigerator.

Joe, wearing a tall chef's hat, stood at the stove for the Main Event: Omelets.

But these weren't just any omelets. These were Omelets *à la* Joe.

Anywhere else—including his own home—Alexander wasn't big on breakfast—but Omelets *à la* Joe were the greatest breakfast meals he had ever eaten.

His heart nearly pounded through his chest when he realized that Joe was calling him over to stand beside him. He'd be *right there* as Joe prepared the mysteriously delicious blend of eggs, cheese, mushrooms, and what Alexander could only imagine was some sort of secret sauce.

All the ingredients were laid out in their own dishes around the stove: the as-yet unbroken eggs, vials of various spices, chopped mushrooms, and, on a back burner, the sauce. Alexander normally *hated* mushrooms, and wouldn't know what to do with spices, but all together, it *worked*.

"Crack open a few eggs for me," Joe commanded, placing a large bowl in front of Alexander, along with a half-empty carton of eggs.

Alexander tried to remember exactly how he'd seen eggs cracked open. Some people tapped them with the blunt edge of a knife, but others, like his own mom and dad, tapped effortlessly at the edge of the bowl.

He picked up an egg, twirling it around a bit as he considered the perfect cracking position.

"Omelet *à la* Joe isn't just about *what* goes into the eggs," Joe offered, "it's all about *how* it goes into the eggs."

Alexander nodded somberly and cracked the first egg on the side of the bowl.

"It's like life," Joe continued. "Some people take every opportunity in their life and do nothing, while others—" he dropped a chunk of butter into the frying pan, "—make the most of what they've got."

...make the most of what they've got.

Alexander felt the egg yolk between his fingers. He'd tranced out again—but only for a second. Luckily, no one noticed. He wiped the yolk off his hands and refocused on cracking eggs. Then he stood by and watched the master at work.

Alexander's parents had brought him once to a Japanese restaurant where the chefs prepared the food in front of the customers on a hot griddle, with knives flying and flames dancing everywhere. Watching Joe at work was almost the same thing, but without the knives. He didn't simply add ingredients; he swept them across the frying pan as if he were waving his hands in a magical incantation, complete with dramatic wafts of steam. With his left hand, Joe added the grated cheese, while his right sprinkled some kind of spice that smelled something like the Indian meal Alexander's parents had brought home a few weeks ago.

When it was all ready, Alexander wasn't shy about using his position as Assistant to the Cook to take first place in line. If they wouldn't have thought him a total pig, he also would have taken three or four helpings right away. Instead, he forced himself to hold back and barely took one.

After balancing off the rest of the plate with a little bit of nearly everything else, Alexander sat down next to Anthony. He couldn't help but smile at Joe.

"You know this is the main reason I come here, right?" Alexander joked.

Joe smiled proudly and nodded. "Thank you."

Anthony poked him.

"You poke too much," Alexander told Anthony, pointing at his plate. "If this wasn't Omelet *à la* Joe, it would be all over you."

Charlie couldn't resist telling Alexander, "He likes to put it on himself," which again sent Eric into hysterics, followed by Ellie and the rest of the family.

Alexander shook his head and tried not to smile. "You people are hopeless." He dug into his eggs and took a mouthful, and everyone laughed again.

Chapter Seven

Make the Most of What You've Got

It was just a thirty-second walk to his own house, but Alexander paused midway to check out the parody video.

It was worse than he imagined. The kids in the video tried to act just like Alexander and Melvin, but with one huge difference. The kid who was supposed to be Alexander was tiny—probably no more than four years old, wearing a gigantic T-shirt with his hair spiked out in a crazy mess and dancing wildly. Somehow they got him to say exactly the things that Alexander had said, in his squeaky, little kid mouse-voice.

"You're not scaring me," the child chanted, "I'm not afraid of you." The boy behind the camera was laughing so hard he couldn't keep the shot level.

That video already had thousands of views. Alexander didn't bother looking at the comments.

If there was one parody video, he knew there would be more.

He tapped off the screen and slid his phone back in his pocket. At least he had a glimmer of hope now, thanks to Joe.

Make the most of what you've got.

Could the solution to all the haters be that simple?

He headed into the house, determined to find out.

The inside of Alexander's house was unlike that of any of his friends—or anyone else for that matter. Tall stacks of books were planted in every conceivable corner, soaring to the ceiling like skyscrapers. There were shelved books, too, but his parents' collection had long since outgrown any sense of order. The school library, with its carefully organized collection, seemed horribly empty in comparison.

Dad was sitting quietly in the middle of everything when Alexander got home, intently checking up and down one precariously balanced stack. He looked up, winked, and said, "Everything good?"

"Yeah."

"How was Anthony's?"

"Good." Alexander crouched down. "What are you looking for?"

Dad somberly surveyed the books scattered around him on the floor. "Inspiration."

Alexander smiled broadly. Sometimes, he thought that he and his dad must have some sort of weird psychic connection because he had the perfect suggestion.

"Omelets," Alexander offered.

Dad looked at him as if he'd said a nonsense word. "Omelets?"

Alexander nodded excitedly. It was all taking shape in his mind, and he was dying to get it out. "It's not about what you have, it's about what you do with it." He watched Dad for a reaction.

"Omelets?" Dad was skeptical.

Alexander was disappointed that Dad didn't get it right away. He stood up to make his point. "Yes, omelets! And what's in the omelets!" He waved his arms back and forth, just like Joe adding his ingredients. "And not just what's in the omelet! See, if you add it in the wrong way, it doesn't come out right, but if you add it in the right way, it's perfect! *Make the most of what you've got!*"

The more he said it, the more sense it made.

"And now," Mom said, emerging from the book-lined hallway, "there are two of you."

Dad looked at Alexander thoughtfully.

Alexander instinctively backed away from both of them. He knew danger when he saw it.

"You should take him to your seminar," Mom said as if it were a point she was making to one of her classes. "Some good father-son bonding."

Father-son bonding? Alexander cringed. Not only did *that* sound entirely awkward, the very idea of seeing one of his dad's seminars—watching him jump around on a stage, telling people to believe in themselves—was nothing less than horrifying.

Dad smiled, though, and Alexander knew his fate was sealed.

"Omelets, Alexander," Dad said with mock drama, nodding as if he understood perfectly. "Omelets."

Alexander threw up his hands in mock frustration and headed for his bedroom. "You don't even know what it means!"

Once inside, he closed his door and turned to the lion mural that filled one entire wall of his room. Teeth bared, forever frozen in mid-pounce, the predator stared down at him with hungry rage.

Alexander thought of the boy looking through the shelves at him in the library, and the stares at lunch.

He considered all of the strange faces calling out "Commando Monkey!" at the mall.

He thought of the comments that told him what everyone was thinking: *Is there something wrong with him?*

Then he thought of omelets.

Omelets à la Joe.

Joe had said—Alexander remembered the exact words—*Some people take every opportunity in their life and do nothing, while others make the most of what they've got.*

Alexander looked over at his closet.

Make the most of what you've got.

He liked the words. They made sense.

Alexander opened the double doors to his closet, and surveyed the floor-to-ceiling jumble inside—a mess of just about everything he'd ever owned, collected, borrowed, or created.

If I'm going to make the most of what I've got, I'd better know what I have.

Alexander moved his laptop over the floor next to the closet, opened up a new document, and typed a heading.

MAKE THE MOST OF WHAT I'VE GOT

He organized his list by categories—clothes, games, models, toys, assorted parts, strange items he couldn't identify, and school things. He found dozens of loose playing cards scattered about, assorted pieces of a magic kit he'd last used when he was nine, and his now-ragged "Leo," a stuffed lion that had once been his constant companion. There was a neatly packed box of toy cars, but almost as many more toy cars on the floor of the closet. His model of the solar system from fourth grade was there, but the wire guides that represented the orbits of the planets were bent out of shape. There were clothes that he'd last worn when he was five, along with a set of rolled-up movie posters.

Vladimir's "racing jacket" was in the closet, too. He'd given it to Alexander when he outgrew it over a year ago. It was bright blue vinyl and covered with sponsor patches like a real racing jacket. If it had been Alexander's in the first place, he would have worn it every day, but it being Vladimir's jacket just made him feel bad. Vladimir was so much bigger now, and Alexander could still fit into the jacket with room to spare.

It wasn't until he had gotten down on his knees to search the floor of his closet that he started to feel hopeful again. He found the white box he'd shoved to the back just a few months before.

He pulled the box into the light.

Make the most of what you've got.

He'd hidden it. Now, he paused before removing the cover.

Its time had come.

Chapter Eight

Boots

Alexander was outside his house early on Monday morning. Usually, Anthony was already waiting for him on the sidewalk, but today was special. Anthony slowed with not-quite-disguised suspicion as he approached. "Hi," he said.

"Hey," Alexander answered as if nothing was unusual.

Anthony's gaze moved down to Alexander's feet. He stared for a few seconds, then looked back up.

"Boots?" he asked cautiously.

Alexander nodded. "Yes," he answered as if it was nothing new. "Hiking boots."

Anthony looked down again.

The boots were thick and heavy and black and reached up over Alexander's ankles. They felt tough and action-filled—almost military tough.

"You don't hike," Anthony said.

When Alexander had seen them on display, surrounded by camouflage, suspended atop a platform above all the other shoes, he knew he wanted them right away.

"I like them," he told Anthony.

That was an understatement. He *loved* them.

Mom and Dad finally bought them for his birthday, after he'd campaigned for them for weeks. At first, he was extremely happy, but when he first put them on and looked in the mirror, his heart sank.

Maybe they'd draw too much attention.

Maybe people would laugh.

He went back to his old shoes, the ones Mom had bought him.

He looks like his mom dresses him.

He placed the boots in their box and kept them hidden in the back of his closet.

Until now.

He decided to wear Vladimir's cool racing jacket, too, and he had a pair of baggy green camouflage shorts he thought would go perfectly with the boots.

Make the most of what you've got.

"Maybe you should wear long pants," Anthony suggested. "Your legs look like toothpicks wearing big clown boots. No offense."

"Well, I like them," Alexander repeated. He'd have to show confidence if this was going to work. He started off in the direction of school. Joe didn't hesitate when he made an omelet, and Alexander wasn't going to hesitate now.

With his ankles encased and unbending in the stiff boots, though, he had to lift his feet higher and try just a little harder to walk. He felt like he was stomping ants all the way down the street.

Anthony laughed.

"You have to work them in," Alexander explained like a pro. "They'll soften up."

He nearly stumbled stepping off the curb, and Anthony laughed again. "Are you sure you don't want to just wear something normal?" he asked.

Alexander stood as tall as he could in the middle of the street and pointed at himself with both thumbs. "*This* is my new normal."

"New normal?" Anthony took a deep, resigned breath.

"It's like your dad's omelets."

Anthony blinked in confusion. "My dad's *omelets?*"

Alexander nodded. "You mix things up a little, you come up with a masterpiece. You make the most of what you've got."

"I *don't* think he meant..." Anthony paused, trying to think of the right words, but only said the obvious, "...big boots."

Alexander stuck his chin out. "You're just going to have to get used to it." He continued across the street.

He heard Anthony laugh but didn't look back.

Vladimir and Darrell were waiting just outside the school gate. Alexander walked right up to them, curious to see how quickly they would notice his boots.

"Hey," he said.

Darrell took one look at Alexander, waited a moment until he knew had everyone's attention, and offered his opinion: "That's the goofiest thing I've ever seen."

Alexander let everyone have their laughs. *They'll get used to it.*

Vladimir seemed transfixed by the boots. "They're huge."

"His feet are huge," Anthony explained calmly. "He's like those little puppies with gigantic paws that are way out of proportion."

"I'm *not* way out of proportion."

Anthony looked thoughtfully at Vladimir. "He's probably going to end up taller than you."

Alexander looked at Vladimir too. It was a long way up.

Darrell shook his head. "You're really going into school like that?"

"There's nothing *wrong* with what I'm wearing."

Darrell just nodded, turned around, and headed through the gate.

Mr. Garcia's classroom wasn't unlocked yet, so they all waited against the lockers. A few feet away, Melvin waited, too. Alexander was careful not to look in his direction. His *Commando Monkey* co-star hadn't said so much as a word to him in weeks.

This time, though, Melvin walked right up to him. He looked down at Alexander's feet. "Nice boots," he said.

Alexander felt relieved. "Thank you!"

"He's joking," Anthony said, nudging Alexander with his elbow.

"Well, *I like them*," Alexander insisted right to Melvin's face, just to show everyone he was confident.

Melvin nodded like Darrell did.

Edgar came bounding down the hall and stopped with an abrupt little jump just by Alexander.

"Hi!"

Edgar followed everyone's gazes down to Alexander's boots. His face brightened. "Nice!"

"Thank you!" Alexander responded, thankful that Edgar, at least, seemed happy for him.

Unfortunately, Edgar then dropped to his knees to inspect the boots more closely. Alexander tolerated it, pretending not to notice that people were staring.

Edgar sprang to his feet, overly excited again. "Those are awesome!"

Everyone laughed.

Ellen reached class just as Garcia opened the door. She looked over at Alexander, looked him up and down for a moment, and then said, "I like it," as she went inside.

Alexander glanced at Darrell. "See?"

"She's being nice," Darrell said as they followed her into the classroom.

"I'm original," Alexander explained, but Darrell ignored him.

Alexander took his seat.

The bell rang.

Garcia didn't start up right away as he usually did.

He stared.

At Alexander's feet.

Until everyone was looking.

"Going off on an *expedition*, Alexander?"

Laughter all around.

Alexander kept his head up and tried to look Garcia straight in the eye.

Show confidence.

Garcia, though, still looked at Alexander's boots, so he tucked his feet back and up under his chair as far as he could. Garcia finally met his gaze but didn't say anything more. He turned away.

Alexander breathed a little easier and let his feet drop.

Clop.

The heavy weight of the boots was too much, and they slapped against the tile. Garcia—and everyone else—turned back to Alexander.

Alexander mumbled, "Sorry," and stared at the top of his desk.

Garcia gazed down at Alexander's boots, grunted, sighed, and headed to the front of the room

Chapter Nine

Those are Interesting

Word traveled fast. By nutrition, sixth graders were already calling him "Commando Monkey Boots!" and trying to take pictures and videos.

Alexander was determined to stay positive, but every few seconds someone walked by the table and snuck a look at his boots. He tried to ignore them, his gaze darting anywhere but in their direction.

But he knew they were there.

Darrell stared at him from across the table. "Those boots have got to go."

Alexander pointed at Darrell's shirt. "Well...that shirt has to go!" There was actually nothing wrong with Darrell's shirt, but he didn't have a better comeback. "And anyway, I like them!"

Anthony turned to him. "Really?"

"Yes, really!"

Anthony paused like he was seriously considering Alexander's response, then suggested, "Maybe you should try for a new new normal."

"What?" Darrell was suddenly interested. "New normal?"

"He wants to change his image," Anthony offered, almost as an apology.

Darrell rolled his eyes at Alexander—an annoying habit Alexander absolutely hated. "You're never going to be normal, *Monkey Boots.*"

"*Commando Monkey Boots*," Vladimir corrected.

"Commando Monkey Boots," Darrell said, nodding. "Sorry."

"Commando Monkey Boots!" Edgar repeated cheerfully as he arrived at the table and forced himself between Alexander and Anthony.

"None of you are funny." Alexander tried to stare down Darrell. "And you're not normal, either!"

Ellen and the artists stopped by the table but didn't sit. Michael actually squatted down to get a better perspective of the boots.

"Those are interesting," he said.

"You *could* say that," Darrell agreed.

Yet again, Alexander said, "I like them." He pointed at Edgar. "And so does he!"

"Yeah!" Edgar agreed with enthusiasm.

"There's nothing wrong with being original," Ellen told Darrell,

"That," Darrell pointed under the table, "isn't original, it's clueless.'"

"If you're so obsessed with my boots," Alexander suggested, "maybe you should get a pair."

Everyone laughed. Alexander felt like he'd scored a point, though he knew Darrell wouldn't just let it go.

"That's a good one," Ellen told Alexander.

Darrell stared at him long and hard. "Do you ever look at yourself in the mirror?"

Even Anthony laughed at that. Was it supposed to be funny? Alexander couldn't tell.

Edgar was all smiles. "You guys are *so* funny."

"I'm not trying to be mean," Darrell continued, "but do you know what you look like? Big boots, big shorts, and that goofy jacket. Seriously, *look in the mirror!*"

Alexander pointed at Vladimir. "It was *his* jacket!"

"When he was little!"

"And people wear camo shorts all the time!" Alexander pointed out.

Darrell wasn't convinced. "Not their dad's!"

"Very funny." Alexander plastered a smile on his face despite his anger. He wouldn't dare admit it, but they were, in fact, his dad's. He had a belt around them—an Army-style fabric belt, too—so it wasn't as if they were falling off. So what if they were a little long?

Darrell wasn't finished. "You look like a little kid."

"Except for his big feet!" Edgar happily added, following Darrell's example and thinking he was being funny, too.

Alexander wanted to tell Darrell off and let him know he was just being a jerk, but maybe everyone would think that he was overreacting.

Like a little kid.

Darrell would tell him he was just playing around, and not to take it so seriously. He'd say it was like a game.

Darrell peered under the table. "You have really bad judgment."

"Will you *stop?*"

Darrell smiled, obviously pleased he'd "won."

As mad as Alexander was at Darrell, though, it wasn't until after lunch that a pug-nosed little sixth grader just about sent him over the edge. With a sneering smile, the boy squatted down, held his phone at boot level, and started shooting video, blocking Alexander's path to algebra class.

When Alexander stopped walking, the kid kept shooting the boots. He didn't even look up. For a moment, Alexander waited for the boy to notice him.

Nothing.

Slowly, Alexander extended his arm toward the boy.

Nothing.

He extended a finger—just a finger—toward the boy's forehead.

Nothing.

Then, with all five fingers, Alexander pressed the boy on his forehead, just enough for him to lose his precarious balance and fall backward.

Sitting on the ground, the surprised boy looked up at Alexander as if to say, *Is there something wrong with you?*

The boy didn't say anything, though. Instead, he aimed his camera directly at Alexander's face, perhaps for the final shot in a new video titled *Commando Monkey Boots Goes Crazy!*

Alexander heard the clicks and beeps of phone cameras all around him. People had stopped moving down the hallway and were staring, trying to figure out what was going on.

A kid was sitting on the ground, and Commando Monkey Boots was standing over him.

Alexander pushed his way through the crowd, hurrying as fast as his boot-heavy feet would carry him.

Chapter Ten

A Complete Encyclopedia of Lions

It wasn't five minutes before he was getting texts from his friends and other schoolmates. They were filled with rumors that he'd punched the kid, thrown food at the kid, poured soda on the kid, or started dancing around like Commando Monkey.

No one got it right, but everyone seemed to have decided he'd gone crazy.

At lunchtime, he opted to avoid the jungle and headed straight to the library.

Library Boy was at his regular table. Mr. Lee nodded at Alexander, noticed his boots, then nodded again, as if he approved. Library Boy looked at the boots, too, but didn't seem impressed, and returned to his reading.

Alexander took a seat at Library Boy's table. There were plenty of other seats all across the library, but somehow it just seemed right to sit there.

With the other weird kid.

Without being too obvious, he glanced at the cover of Library Boy's closed notebook and studied the upside-down name.

"Hey, Colin."

Library Boy—Colin—gave him only a passing glance and returned to the large, illustrated book before him.

"I love that book," Alexander said.

Colin looked up for an even briefer instant as if he was nervous.

Alexander could tell he was suspicious, but it was true—he'd recognized the large, glossy pages right away: *A Complete Encyclopedia of Lions.*

There were hundreds of photos, and thousands of facts—he could read it endlessly. When he was younger and teachers asked such things, lions were his go-to favorite animals.

"I'd love to see them in the wild someday," he told Colin.

For a few seconds, Colin didn't respond at all. Then he closed the book and covered it with another one.

Alexander sat back in his chair. Feeling awkward, he pulled his science textbook out of his backpack and randomly paged through it for a few seconds. Then he looked at Colin again.

"Did you know that they can run fifty miles an hour?" he asked.

At first, Colin didn't say anything. His head was still down, staring at the closed books in front of him.

Alexander looked back at his textbook, thumbing through the pages and studying the page numbers. He never realized that it had over four hundred pages.

Just above a whisper, Colin asked, "Did you know you can hear a lion roar five miles away?"

Alexander looked at Colin, softening his voice, too. "They can leap thirty-six feet."

"They hunt together, like a team," Colin responded, his voice fading so much that Alexander could barely hear him. "That's why they're the best."

Colin ducked his head down, rearranged his books again, and re-opened his lion book as if nothing had happened.

Alexander waited, but it seemed as if Colin had forgotten he was there.

Alexander tried one more time. "I have this lion mural on one whole wall of my bedroom."

Colin ignored him.

Alexander's phone buzzed—a text from Anthony.

Are you okay?

Alexander texted back and told him that he was okay.

Where are you? Did you get in trouble?

He answered no, but Anthony wouldn't let it go.

Was it Darrell? Don't let him get you mad.

Colin got up to talk to Mr. Lee.

Alexander answered Anthony.

I'm not, I just don't feel good.

Colin and Mr. Lee disappeared between two shelves. Anthony kept texting. **Why don't you feel good?**

I just don't.

Alexander thought for a moment that he'd satisfied Anthony's curiosity.

Then Anthony called.

Alexander quickly ducked out of the library to answer.

"Are you sick? What do you have?"

"I just don't feel good."

"Well, what are the symptoms?" Anthony sounded concerned.

Do you have to overreact about everything?

"Don't worry about it."

"Alexander, tell me."

Anthony sounded like his mother, and Alexander knew he wouldn't stop until he got an answer. He looked around to make sure there was no one nearby that would hear him and said the first thing that came into his head.

"I have diarrhea."

Anthony paused a moment, and Alexander hoped that was the end of it.

"You should drink a lot of water," Anthony advised.

"Thanks, *Mom.*"

"And you shouldn't have fruit or milk."

"Fine."

He heard Vladimir ask what was wrong, and Anthony announcing *to everyone* that Alexander had diarrhea.

"Well, I have to go to the bathroom again, so I've got to go." Alexander ended the call and wished he had thought of something else.

Chapter Eleven

I Don't Have Big Feet

Just before Alexander walked into science class, Mom called.

"You have diarrhea?"

"Did Anthony call you?" Alexander asked in disbelief.

"His mother did. Are you okay?"

"I'm fine. I have to go to class."

"Do you want to come home?"

"I'm okay."

"Drink plenty of water, understand? You don't want to get dehydrated. Was it something you ate?"

"I have to go, bye!"

"Are you okay?" Vladimir asked as soon as Alexander walked into the classroom.

"I'm *fine*," Alexander said, secretly wanting to yell, *I don't have diarrhea.*

Just before he sat down at the desk he shared with Paul, Ellen walked right up to him. "Are you all right?"

"I'm fine," he told her, hoping she was just seeing something in his expression.

"You should drink a lot of water," she advised, pausing for a moment until Alexander barely managed a thank-you.

Ellen finally went back to her seat. Alexander felt his cheeks burning.

Mr. Shek looked right at him. For an instant, Alexander thought he might make a comment about his red face, but instead, he called him to the front of the room, took him by the shoulders, and turned him to face everyone.

"Boots!" Shek exclaimed to the class, and all eyes gazed down at Alexander's feet. Again, people laughed.

"Even boots have science behind them!" Shek declared.

Alexander gazed longingly at his empty seat. Why did so many teachers care about his boots?

Shek pointed at the boots as if they were the greatest invention in all civilization, "Boots are *all about* energy—preserving it, leveraging it, and, if you don't have the right boots, even *wasting* it."

People were laughing—at him, Alexander was sure, and not at Shek's half-baked joke.

Shek grabbed a chair and set it in front of Alexander. "Put your foot up!"

He looked at Shek pleadingly, but Shek insisted, and Alexander swung his right foot atop the chair. The height of the boot meant he couldn't bend his ankle, so he had to lift his leg higher than usual. He could barely keep his balance and had to hold his arms out like he was on a balance beam just to keep from falling over.

More people were laughing, but Shek was oblivious and just kept on lecturing, lost in excitement as he talked about how the sole, the laces, the tongue, linings, paddings, and who knew what else worked together to help the hiker keep hiking.

Finally, Shek was through and told Alexander he could sit down. He was in such an awkward position, though, he had to grab his ankle to pull his heavy boot off the chair, generating even more laughter.

He sat back down as Shek introduced the lab assignment.

Paul leaned back in his chair to get a closer look at the boots. Alexander tried to ignore him, staring off at the table of elements on the wall behind Shek.

The task, Shek explained, was to use a selection of paper, cardboard, Styrofoam, and other materials to create some sort of enclosure to keep an egg from cracking open when dropped from several feet onto the ground.

The outcome of the assignment/competition (everything in Shek's class was a competition) was already certain—Alexander and his lab partner Paul would end up on top. People in class were already starting to call them the mad scientists.

Paul, though, who was usually all business with their science projects, was more interested in Alexander's boots.

Alexander started pulling the egg drop supplies out of the plastic bag. "I think we should start with the Styrofoam."

"Those are big."

"They're hiking boots."

"They're *big* hiking boots."

Alexander held up a Styrofoam slab, but Paul interrupted before he had a chance to say anything.

"They must be big on you."

"They fit," Alexander insisted.

"Really?"

Alexander waved the Styrofoam slab at him. "We have fifteen minutes."

"Where do you hike?"

Paul leaned back to look at Alexander's boots again. Alexander tucked them under his chair.

"You must have big feet," Paul speculated.

He felt like throwing the Styrofoam at Paul. "*I don't have big feet!*"

Suddenly, the class was completely silent.

From the far side of the room, Shek explained a simple scientific fact: "Alexander, you *do* have big feet."

Chapter Twelve

You Should Go Now

Paul finally focused on the eggs instead of the boots, and—no surprise to Alexander—they won the competition. Their Styrofoam-bubble-wrapped orb was the only container in the entire class to survive a drop from six feet up.

Alexander was secretly proud but kept it to himself.

Just a minute before the end of science class, while everyone was gathering together their books, Shek called Alexander and Paul to his desk.

"I didn't do anything," Alexander offered right away. All he wanted to do was get across campus to his last class, and then he'd be done with one of the worst days of his life. He didn't need any delays.

Shek raised his eyebrows in surprise but didn't correct him. He leisurely shuffled the papers on his desk and set them aside in a nice little pile.

The bell rang, and everyone else rushed into the hall.

Alexander looked anxiously at the wall clock behind Shek.

"Don't worry, I'll write you a note," Shek assured him.

Shek wasn't in any hurry, though. He told them both about a citywide science competition, and how he wanted them to take part.

Alexander looked at Paul, who was nodding at the idea as if he were interested.

The winners of that contest, Shek continued, would get to go to New York City and compete against teams from schools around the entire country.

To Alexander's infinite frustration, Paul started asking questions—when, where, what would they actually have to do? Shek carefully—slowly—answered.

Alexander considered grabbing an egg out of the nearby carton and gagging Paul so he would shut up. Did they really have to talk about this *now?*

Kids started coming in for Shek's next class, and it wasn't until the bell rang to start the *next* class that he finally wrote excuse slips and sent Paul and Alexander on their way.

The halls were totally empty.

To get to history class, Alexander walked across the lunch area and entered the building, stepping off the concrete pathways outside and into the tiled hallway. With classes already underway, he could hear only one sound—his boots.

Clop-clop.

It was impossible to walk softly—the boots were just too heavy. He was getting tired, too. With a million kids around, it didn't matter. Alone in the hallway, he practically echoed off the walls.

Clop-clop-clop.

In a classroom somewhere nearby, a boy heard him and whinnied like a horse. Several classrooms responded with laughter.

Alexander opened the door to his history class, ready to present his excuse slip. Mrs. Blake looked up from taking roll.

Before she had a chance to say anything, a kid Alexander didn't know declared loudly, "We heard you coming a mile away."

Alexander walked up to Mrs. Blake and handed her Shek's excuse slip, then turned and sat at his desk, careful not to look at anyone else.

He knew they were looking at him. According to the clock above Mrs. Blake's head, he had fifty more minutes left.

Then what?

Walk home with his friends? Pretend nothing had happened? Let Darrell embarrass him? Argue? Alexander couldn't imagine walking home with everyone and listening to Darrell go on and on about the boots.

"Alexander!"

He looked up. Mrs. Blake was glaring at him. "You can stop that," she said.

At first, Alexander had no idea what she was talking about, and then he realized he had a pencil in his hand. He couldn't be sure, but he thought he might have been tapping it on the desk.

He put the pencil down, pressing his hand on top of it as if it would tap by itself.

More laughter.

Colin had it easy. His entire school day was limited to the library. He never had to deal with kids judging him, or laughing at him, or talking down to him. He just sat in the library and did his work.

Maybe Alexander could do that.

Edgar, seated three rows ahead, was turned around in his seat, watching him. Alexander tried to give him a look that said *turn back*, but it was too late.

"Edgar!"

Edgar's head whipped back toward Mrs. Blake.

"Don't stare at Alexander!"

More laughter.

The lights dimmed and Mrs. Blake put on a video. Alexander hadn't paid attention to her introduction and had no idea what he was about to see. He just hoped it would last the entire forty-five minutes until the end of the day.

Black and white footage of planes and missiles, tanks and walls, and three huge words filled the screen:

THE COLD WAR

Alexander opened his notebook and picked up his pen because everyone else did.

He could sense that the narrator in the video was declaring something important and dramatic, but he wasn't listening. He thought of Colin instead, hiding out in the library.

Maybe he could lay low for a while. People would forget about Commando Monkey—and the boots.

After the last bell rang, Alexander darted out of the classroom before Edgar had a chance to follow, and headed straight for the library.

Just as he expected, Colin was still at his regular table, while Mr. Lee pushed a cart around and re-shelved books.

Alexander sat across from Colin.

"Hi."

Colin looked up and acknowledged him with a nod, but didn't say anything.

"Can I ask you something?"

Colin looked up again and waited.

Alexander looked around to make sure Mr. Lee wasn't nearby. He leaned forward to whisper, "Why are you in here all the time?"

Colin didn't answer at first, and Alexander felt guilty for asking.

"You don't have to answer," he added quickly.

Colin ran his fingers across a scratch on the table. "I just like it."

Alexander didn't believe him.

"Do you take all of your classes in here?"

Colin shrugged. He looked nervous.

Mr. Lee came over. "Alexander, is there anything I can help you find?"

"No, I was just talking—"

"Then you should be heading home. Don't bother Colin."

"I'm not bothering—"

"You should go now."

Colin ducked his head again. Alexander looked from Colin to Mr. Lee and back again.

He'd never been scolded by Mr. Lee.

Mr. Lee waited, almost like he was standing guard.

"I'll see you later," Alexander told an unresponsive Colin, then stood up and grabbed his backpack.

"*Go*, Alexander," Mr. Lee insisted.

Feeling weirdly embarrassed that he'd somehow offended Mr. Lee, he grabbed his backpack and left. After stopping by his locker to pick up his math book, he headed out the north gate.

An old red pickup truck was rattling at the curb. He couldn't see the driver, but standing by the passenger door, holding the door open as Colin climbed inside, was Mr. Lee. He shut the door, waved to the driver, and started back toward the school gate as the truck sputtered down the street.

Mr. Lee paused for a moment when he saw Alexander, considered him for a moment, then walked right past him.

Colin, Alexander realized, was on lockdown.

Chapter Thirteen

Scrawny

All the way home, Alexander got texts and even calls from his friends—even Darrell.

He ignored them all.

It was going to be a late night for Mom and Dad, so the house was entirely quiet by the time he got home. He didn't bother turning anything on; he went straight to his bedroom.

For the second time that day, Alexander struggled to unlace his boots. Once he slipped them off, he felt like he'd been freed from chains, and he rubbed his ankles to restore some circulation. One boot sat upright, the other was on its side. The box still lay open just outside his closet.

The person who commented that he looked like his mom dressed him was wrong. He could dress *stupidly* all by himself.

He thought he might feel better if he took a shower.

He stepped in and tried not to think of anything, but his mind kept racing. The water sprayed onto the top of his head.

Is there something wrong with him?
What is he, six?
Mutant.
Scrawny, isn't he?
Scrawny.

Not only were there over two million people laughing at him because of the *Commando Monkey* video, his friends (Darrell, especially) were ridiculing him, and random kids were harassing him. Now even *Mr. Lee* had chased him away.

And it wasn't so much that he felt like the most awkward person he could imagine, but thanks to the video, he knew everyone else felt that way about him, too.

Ellen was friendly about it, but maybe she was just being nice. Not even one comment called him original. Hundreds, though, called him weird.

Maybe Joe was wrong. The ingredients *did* matter. Even *he* couldn't make an omelet with a rotten egg.

Alexander got out of the shower and dried off as fast as he could. He forced himself to look in the mirror.

He tried to flex his arms, but it was hopeless.

Scrawny, isn't he?
How do you make the most of what you've got if you've got nothing?

He stormed out of the bathroom without even bothering to pick up his towel, then found the hallway back to his bedroom blocked—

—by Mom and Dad.

They'd come home early.

They looked at him, clearly confused. Mom had a bottle of pink liquid in her right hand.

"Are you okay?" Mom asked.

"Um..." was all Alexander could manage. He backed up into the bathroom and grabbed his towel, trying to act casual despite everything.

Safely covered, he faced his parents and nodded at the bottle. "What's that?"

"It's for your...condition."

"I don't have a condition."

Then he remembered.

"I know it's a little embarrassing..." Mom began.

He held up his hands to stop her. "Mom, I'm okay. I don't need to have," he tried to remember the name of the pink stuff, but couldn't, *"that."*

Dad crouched down, an obvious ploy to be on his level. "Come on, it's not like it tastes that bad."

"It was a *joke*," Alexander insisted, believing that it was close enough to the truth.

Mom looked doubtful.

He had to think quickly. "It was sort of a prank on Anthony. I didn't think he'd tell his mom."

Mom and Dad considered his explanation.

"You're sure?" Dad asked, still looking concerned.

Alexander made sure to look him in the eye. "Yes."

Mom and Dad looked at him.

Alexander retightened his towel, squeezed between his parents, and headed for his room.

Chapter Fourteen

Everything Good?

Alexander wasn't exactly in the mood to go with his dad to his seminar trip the next day, but school was the alternative, so he didn't argue.

The drive down to the hotel in Santa Monica took way too long. Traffic crawled almost the entire way, and Alexander felt self-conscious sitting next to his father. He kept his earbuds in the entire time, listening to music so that Dad wouldn't try to talk to him and bond. He'd put his phone on "airplane mode" so that he couldn't get any texts or phone calls from his friends. He still hadn't answered anyone, and he really didn't want to.

As soon as they drove up to the hotel, a gaggle of people whom Alexander thought were like just like adult *Edgars* came up to Dad and greeted him like he was a celebrity. Someone in a hotel uniform carried in their bags as the gaggle thanked Dad for coming and told him how they expected a good crowd. Dad introduced

Alexander, and he smiled on cue and shook hands with everyone.

Some old guy reached out and ruffled Alexander's hair as if he was a toddler. "You look just like your dad, do you know that?"

Obviously, that's because I'm his son!

Alexander said nothing, concentrating every bit of his energy on keeping up his smile.

Eventually, the gaggle turned their attention back to Dad and swept him away through the automatic sliding doors.

Alexander held back just a moment, noticing, for the first time, the large placard sitting on an easel next to the valet station. The placard featured Dad's name and picture, and, in big letters, the question he asked Alexander every day: *Everything Good?*

It was the title of Dad's book and his favorite phrase.

Stepping into the dark, sleek lobby—it had large monitors with abstract designs, and red and blue LEDs glowing everywhere—Alexander paused for a moment, then spotted Dad at the check-in counter. The gaggle was already walking away. Dad finished checking in and waved Alexander over.

"After the seminar, what do you say we go out for a night on the town?" Dad asked.

Night on the town.

Alexander smiled politely.

"We'll hang out!" Dad said.

Hang out.

What could he say?

He said nothing.

They would undoubtedly be talking.

It wasn't that he didn't like talking to his dad or being with him. Lately, though, it just made him nervous, and he wasn't entirely sure why.

After the seminar, as Mom said, they'd have some *bonding time.*

They went upstairs. Dad changed into what he called his presentation suit, and he made Alexander change, too, into nice pants, dress shoes, and a white dress shirt. Since he wasn't on stage, he didn't much see the point, but he did it anyway.

Back downstairs, they entered the auditorium through a door behind the raised stage. There were hundreds of people, and they all erupted in wild cheers the moment Dad, after adjusting his microphone-headset, bounded up onto the raised stage.

Alexander stayed back, hidden from the audience behind fake shrubbery masking the stairs up to the platform.

Dad screamed to the audience, "EVERYTHING GOOD?" which sent them off into more cheers. Alexander stepped even deeper into the shrubbery, to make certain nobody could see him. Dad could be hyper sometimes, but this was off the charts.

Dad answered his own question: "YES, EVERYTHING'S GOOD!"

Another round of cheers and applause thundered through the room.

Dad stopped screaming but still ran around the stage, his hands moving wildly as he started off on his "Believe in Yourself" stuff. Alexander didn't listen too closely, focusing instead on the creaking metal of the portable stage as Dad stomped across it. He watched Dad's pacing feet, his waving arms, and his sweating face as he told everyone what they wanted to hear. Alexander's gaze wandered up to the row of ceiling-mounted spotlights trained on his father and wondered who controlled them.

In an instant, though, one word turned his attention squarely back on Dad.

"OMELETS!"

Dad screamed it out like he'd screamed out "EVERYTHING GOOD!" and then said, "I was talking to my son Alexander the other day..."

He gestured for Alexander to join him.

You can't be serious!

Dad gestured again and waited, creating an awkward pause. Alexander felt compelled to walk up the metal stairs onto the stage. He wished he were still six, so he could have a temper tantrum and run away, but he held it together.

Barely.

The room applauded, though Alexander wasn't sure why. Dad whispered for him to wave hi, so he gave them a stiff wave, and they applauded again. He started to turn to the stairs, ready to get off the stage, but Dad put his arm around his shoulder and kept him there so everyone could keep staring.

Scrawny, isn't he?

"Omelets are like people. Do you know why? It's not about what you have, it's how you put it all together!" Dad quoted Alexander precisely. "If you add it in the wrong way, it doesn't come out right, but if you add it in the right way, it's *perfect!* It's that simple!"

Alexander couldn't help but stare up in astonishment at his dad.

No, it's not that simple!

"Make the most of what you've got!" Dad shouted to the crowd.

More cheers.

Finally, Dad lifted his arm away and Alexander beat a hasty retreat off the platform, slipped out the back door through which they had entered, and charged out of the hotel.

Chapter Fifteen

Slimy and Smelly

Alexander headed down to the Santa Monica Pier, just a block away from the hotel. The pier wasn't a small fishing platform; it was a huge world of its own, with a mini-amusement park, souvenir stands, street performers, and a giant, brightly lit Ferris wheel dominating the sky above. Alexander felt drawn to its swirling, animated designs. He would have taken a ride, but his money was still in his other pants. He could only wander around the crowded pier and watch other people as they had *their* fun.

There were lots of families, and endless crowds of kids around his age, too—though they seemed to get along with each other better than he did with *his* friends lately.

Alexander leaned up against a wooden railing, not far from a caricature artist. He watched the short man create cartoons for several tourists—an old man, a young couple, and a little girl. In each case, he asked them what they were interested in, or what they did for a living, and he made it part of the cartoon. The old man was a veteran, and the artist drew him riding atop a World War II plane. The young couple was visiting from England, and he drew them waving a huge British flag over the pier. The girl's drawing had her riding a pink pony.

Alexander wasn't sure what he'd want in his picture. Riding a lion? Hunched over a computer? The first choice sounded stupid; the other, boring. Of course, if it was a caricature of his true self, maybe he'd be dancing around like Commando Monkey.

With boots.

The artist wouldn't have much to work with.

After finishing his cartoon of the little girl, the light had faded, and the artist packed up his supplies and headed off the pier. Alexander turned and peered over the railing down to the beach, where swimmers were shaking off towels and heading back to their cars, and families and small groups of friends were strolling just beyond the rising tide.

Then he saw a boy, maybe ten years old, walking by himself along the beach. Unlike most people, he wore his shoes despite the sand, and he had on regular street clothes instead of a bathing suit. He obviously hadn't been swimming. He didn't look lost, but he didn't fit in, either. He wasn't just going for a walk, he was heading somewhere. He didn't even look at the ocean.

As the boy moved closer to the pier, heading directly underneath him, Alexander noticed that the boy's clothes were caked with grime. He disappeared below the pier.

Maybe he'd just been playing in the sand.

Alexander ran to the other side of the pier, to see if he could get another look at the boy, just make sure he was okay.

But he didn't show up.

He was probably just playing.

But what if he wasn't?

What if Alexander was the only person to see something odd about the kid? What if the boy was in trouble? What if he was a runaway?

Alexander decided he'd better check it out, just in case. It was getting dark. Midway up the pier, there was a stairway down to the beach. He flew down the steps and onto the sand.

When he reached the area beneath where he had been standing, though, the shadows made it difficult to identify anyone. There were more people than Alexander had expected, walking under the pier in the dry sand or exploring the shallow water, collecting sand crabs, running between the pier supports, and dodging the little waves.

If the kid was a runaway, maybe he could take him to a cop somewhere so they could get him home. If he was a runaway, though, maybe he wouldn't want to go to a cop. Alexander would have to just go and tell the cop about the kid.

Maybe he could just buy the kid some food, or give him a few dollars or something. He had no idea—and no money, anyway.

What did runaway kids do? Where did they go? Once, when he and Anthony were very small, they talked about running away but hadn't really thought about it much. It just seemed like an adventure.

In an instant, a sudden large wave splashed against Alexander, throwing him off his feet and soaking his dress shirt, his dress shoes, and his good pants. He pulled himself from a tangled mass of oily seaweed and caught a strong whiff of something dead and fishy. He reached up and pulled a revolting clump of gray goop from his hair.

After struggling to his feet, Alexander stumbled out from under the pier and back up the beach, finally reaching the crosswalk at the street by the pier. His clothes were sticking to him, and he felt sand everywhere.

Other people were waiting for the crossing signal, too. They all turned the moment Alexander arrived to see what smelled so bad.

A kid looked at him, and Alexander realized right away that it was the "runaway" boy, who obviously wasn't a runaway at all. He was standing with his parents, looking at Alexander as if *he* were a gross-looking runaway. After a moment, the boy's expression brightened, and he tugged at his dad's shirt and pointed.

"Commando Monkey!"

Thankfully, the light changed, and Alexander hurried ahead of everyone across the street and back to the hotel. He didn't want to walk through the lobby of the hotel looking the way he did, so he made his way through the parking structure and entered through the back way. A few people were waiting for the elevators, but once he approached, they all stepped back and let him ride alone.

He didn't blame them.

At the hotel room, Alexander slid his keycard through the door lock. He could already imagine being in the shower.

The door didn't open.

He tried again.

Nothing.

He pressed down on the door lever, just to make sure.

He checked the room number. It was correct.

He slid the keycard again.

The little red light in the door was supposed to turn green, and the door was supposed to unlock.

It didn't.

He knocked.

"Dad?"

Nothing.

He knocked louder.

"Dad?"

He slid the keycard again. It still didn't work.

Seawater—now dripping into a spreading puddle beneath his feet—had ruined his keycard.

He'd have to go back downstairs, find Dad, and get the other one.

Alexander decided to take the stairs this time. He'd figured he'd probably stunk up the elevators enough. Six floors weren't that bad, and it was all going down, anyway.

By the time he'd gotten back to the first floor, he was beginning to feel itchy. He started to scratch everywhere and couldn't stop. He had to pass through the bank of elevators to get to the lobby and caught sight of himself in the mirror-lined walls.

His pants were caked with sand, his once-white shirt was streaked with green algae, and his hair was matted down and slimy. He barely recognized himself.

He stepped into the darkened lobby. With the soft bluish glow distorting everything, it was hard to spot Dad. He could be in any corner, sitting at any of the little islands of sofas spread across the lobby, or maybe in the bar tucked off to the side.

Alexander pulled his phone out of his front pocket and tried to turn it on. It was totally dead—another seawater victim.

He wandered around the room, hovering near every sofa, trying to recognize his father. He was grateful that people couldn't see him clearly but as quiet as he tried to be, they still smelled him coming.

He couldn't help but scratch more furiously; his skin felt like it was crawling with little bugs. He clawed at his arms, his stomach, his legs—even his butt. He felt like he was going insane.

He stood by the wide entranceway to the bar and peered in. Even his back was itching now, precisely where he couldn't reach. Alexander rubbed his back against a corner of the short barrier wall that separated the bar from the rest of the lobby, but it only gave him limited relief.

A shadowy shape hurried up to him. From the glint of the little brass badge, Alexander figured it was hotel staff.

Finally.

"Excuse me." The voice was nasal—and not friendly. "You're going to have to leave."

Alexander stopped rubbing his back and faced the dark figure looming above him.

"I'm staying here," he offered quietly, "with my dad."

The snooty man seemed to sniff the air. "I don't think so." He took out a handkerchief and covered his nose.

Embarrassed, Alexander pulled out his keycard to prove he belonged, but the man snatched it from his hand.

"You're going to need to leave." Snooty made a twirling motion with his finger, pointed to the entrance, and called out, "Security!"

Stay calm.

Alexander searched the lobby again for his dad, but only saw the seminar sign with his father's picture.

He pointed at it and pleaded, "I'm staying here with my dad."

"Oh, really?" Snooty was clearly doubtful.

The guard joined them. "You don't want us to call the police, do you?" he asked. He kept his distance, which was fine with Alexander.

Smelling bad had its advantages.

Alexander stepped closer to the guard, and the guard took a step back.

"Do whatever you want," Alexander answered, feeling a touch braver. He folded his arms across his chest so he wouldn't start scratching.

The guard took out his phone.

Alexander considered making a run for it and waiting for Dad somewhere outside, but wasn't sure where he could go. Instead, he stood his ground. He could feel a seawater puddle squishing on the carpet beneath his feet.

Hotel guests made wide circles around him, while Snooty watched with disgust.

Alexander's entire body was screaming to get scratched. He kept his arms tightly folded.

In a few minutes, two muscular, stern-looking police officers walked through the sliding glass doors, pausing so their eyes could adjust to the dim lobby.

Now what?

Alexander's heart was pounding.

Where is Dad?

If Dad were there, he'd walk right up to them, look the officers in the eye, and shake their hands.

Even if he looked like I do.

With a big smile on his face, Alexander walked right up to the startled officers and extended his hand. "Hi!"

He shook the first officer's hand, grasping it with both hands as his dad would, and reading the man's badge. "Officer Fisher!" He did the same with the other officer. "Officer Marquez!"

Snooty scurried up to the officers and told them, "He doesn't belong here."

The officers looked at Alexander, trying to understand. Smelly, gross, and polite probably didn't go together too often.

"I'm staying at this hotel." He pointed at Snooty. "And he wants to throw me out!"

Snooty looked down at Alexander, gesturing at him as if he were shooing away a fly. "He's not one of our guests."

Alexander pointed at the *Everything Good?* sign. "My father did a seminar."

Sergeant Marquez glanced at the sign and turned to Snooty. "And you can't look that up?"

Snooty sniffed again at Alexander's horrible stink, and nodded at the sign. "He saw that and claimed that was his father. It's a common trick." He bent down and sneered at Alexander, "Our guests don't come off the streets."

"I was at the *beach*," he firmly told Snooty. "I fell in."

Snooty was unmoved. "Next time, wear a bathing suit." He gave Alexander a croaking laugh.

The officers looked at Alexander. He shrugged at them as if to say, *I don't know why he's saying those crazy things.*

They smiled back.

There was a commotion near the door—a crowd was passing through.

"Dad!"

Finally.

Dad came over, surrounded by a cluster of Edgars.

"Do you know this boy?" Officer Marquez asked.

Dad looked Alexander up and down, and then sniffed.

"This is my son." He took in Alexander's condition again. "A version of him, anyway."

The Edgars laughed.

"What's going on here?" Dad asked.

"*He* wanted to throw me out," Alexander explained.

Dad looked at Snooty, almost smiling. "And you called the police?"

Snooty stuttered for an explanation, but Dad didn't wait for one. He introduced himself to the officers, and shook their hands just as Alexander had done.

Satisfied that everything was okay, Officers Fisher and Marquez excused themselves and left.

Alexander started toward the lobby counter. "Do you think I can get a new card now?" he asked. Just to sound classy, he added, "Please?"

He could tell Snooty wanted to say something unkind to him, but instead he walked over to the counter. He created a new keycard in seconds and handed it over. "Now *please* go upstairs."

Alexander smiled. "Thank you."

Dad patted him on the back. "Class act," he said, and pulled off a dry piece of seaweed.

One of the Edgars, a woman in a blue business suit, looked at Alexander and nodded at the others solemnly. "Make the most of what you've got."

Chapter Sixteen

They Look Up to You

Alexander felt convinced—one hundred percent positive—that he and Dad would have their father-son Bonding Talk at dinner that evening. While he wasn't exactly certain what that talk would be like, he was pretty sure it wasn't the *What a Day!* talk it turned out to be.

Since Mom had said this would be a Bonding Trip, he'd been trying to figure out exactly what that meant. When he looked it up online, all he could find were descriptions of activities a kid and his dad could do together. Alexander and his father didn't qualify in any category, actually. They didn't play ball together. They didn't go to a car show together. They never went camping together.

At dinner, he began to wonder if the bonding talk might be the *other* kind of talk—the embarrassing one he'd heard about but never experienced.

The only thing that happened after dinner, though, was dessert.

By the time they started driving home the next day, Alexander felt like he'd somehow escaped the bonding thing altogether.

Then they stepped into the house.

"And how did it go?" Mom asked, her gaze searching Alexander and then his dad. He knew right off that she wasn't talking about the seminar.

Dad patted him on the shoulder and told her, "It went great!" He looked directly at Alexander and added, "Good bonding."

What?

Alexander couldn't help but stare at Dad—he felt like he was onstage at the hotel again.

"Right?"

Alexander nodded. "Yeah." Then he realized that it wasn't about any talk at all.

It was the experience.

Dad told his audience of one—Mom—how Alexander had dealt with the hotel staffer. On the way home, he'd told Alexander how proud he was, but now, in front of Mom, the story was taking on epic proportions. The way Dad was talking, Alexander felt like he'd faced down the entire hotel.

And won.

Ten minutes after he'd gone back to his bedroom to unpack, though, Mom called from the front of the house.

"Family meeting!"

Leaving them alone to talk was never a good idea.

Usually, a family meeting meant he was in trouble and was about to be interrogated. Alexander figured he was going to get yelled at for ruining his phone. He had a pretty solid argument, though. It was an honest accident. It wasn't as if he was going swimming and forgot he had it in his pocket. He couldn't predict that a giant wave would suddenly smash into him.

He entered Mom's office. She was seated behind her big, old-fashioned oak desk, and Dad was sitting in one of the two chairs facing her. Alexander took the empty one next to Dad.

"I'm sorry about the phone," he offered quickly, thinking he would cool them down with an apology before they had a chance to lecture.

"This isn't about your phone," Dad said, sounding as if it were something much more serious.

"This is about Anthony," Mom said.

Alexander felt his heart jump. "Is he okay?"

"He's fine," Mom assured him, softening her voice. "He called this morning, wondering if you were okay."

Alexander shrugged as if he had no idea why Anthony would call.

"Why haven't you called him back?" Dad asked.

"My phone—"

"He said you haven't talked to him in *two* days?"

Mom wasn't buying it.

He had to think fast. He couldn't exactly explain that he didn't want to speak to Anthony because he didn't want to speak to Darrell, and if he talked to Anthony he would have to speak to Darrell, too. It wouldn't make sense.

It wasn't making a lot of sense to him, either.

"Call him," Mom insisted.

Dad offered his own phone. "Call him."

Alexander felt cornered. He took the phone.

They watched him.

He looked at the phone.

"I need to get his number."

He actually knew Anthony's phone number but escaped to his room for some privacy. After a few seconds of hesitating, he dialed.

Anthony picked up. "Hello?"

"Hey."

There was a slight pause, and then Anthony said, "Hey," as if nothing had happened.

Alexander wasn't sure where to go from there.

Anthony did. "You're coming over, right?"

"Huh?"

"It's Charlie and Eric's birthday."

"Oh, yeah, of course," Alexander replied, having forgotten completely. "When?"

Anthony laughed. "Now!"

Relieved that Anthony hadn't asked any questions, Alexander grabbed two long-wrapped presents from under his bed and headed over to Anthony's house.

The twins gave Alexander a brotherly group hug as soon as he got there, and they seemed to like his gifts. He'd bought both of them cases for their tablets but made sure they weren't perfectly identical. He wanted them to know he didn't think of them as exactly the same, even though they looked the same. When they saw that their covers were different, they showed them off to each other and laughed, then hugged Alexander again.

"They look up to you," Joe told him.

Alexander shrugged. "At least somebody does," he said. He saw Anthony frown for just an instant before he realized it was a joke.

Alexander couldn't stay long. It was a school night, after all, and there wouldn't be a sleepover. Anthony walked with him to the front door, but instead of just saying goodbye, he stepped outside with Alexander and shut the door behind them.

"Darrell thinks you're mad at him," he said.

Alexander looked anxiously down the street as his house. Wasn't that obvious?

"You should call him," Anthony suggested.

Alexander held out his empty hands. "I don't have a phone, remember?"

Anthony sighed. Alexander got the message: It was a lame excuse.

Just before he headed home, Anthony tried once more to talk to his friend, who hadn't said a word in fifteen minutes.

"Do me one little favor."

This was the kind of moment where Alexander was used to taking out his phone and distracting himself.

But he didn't have his phone, so he offered a reluctant, "What?"

"Just work it out."

CHAPTER SEVENTEEN

THE DARRELL QUESTION

Just work it out?

The first thing that Alexander tried to figure out on the way home was, *Why is it up to me?*

And it wasn't just Darrell, either. It wasn't as if Alexander was reacting to people—they were reacting to him. It was almost as if people knew something he didn't about the way things worked—like they were speaking some strange language he didn't understand.

Tomorrow, he'd have to go right back into the middle of it.

And he'd have to deal with Darrell.

Even if he didn't want to talk to him, he would have to deal with him.

All night long, he tossed and turned, working out a mental list of everything that could happen.

He *could* try to *work it out* with Darrell, but who knew how Darrell would react?

Darrell could catch him off guard and speak up first, and make some comment about Alexander refusing to talk to him, which could be bad if he didn't have a comeback ready (and he usually didn't).

There was always the option of avoiding Darrell entirely. He'd avoid him before school, in class, and at lunch. Unless he could convince everyone else to do the same thing, though, Alexander thought that he might end up alone.

He could try to get revenge on Darrell for all the things he said to him, but Alexander wasn't good at that sort of thing, so he'd probably just make a fool of himself.

If he did talk to Darrell, what would he say? He doubted Darrell would apologize for anything—in fact, Alexander was convinced that Darrell believed he was right, and Alexander was just a little kid.

Maybe it just wasn't possible to stay friends with Darrell.

He decided that he needed to tell Darrell to find other friends. He could even think of a few ways to say it, too.

You need to find other friends,

or

You don't like me, and I don't like you, so you need to find other friends,

or

Since you don't want to treat me like a friend, you need to stay away,

or

If you think you can talk to me like that, you're wrong.

The more Alexander thought of what he might say, the angrier he got imagining how Darrell might react.

There you are again, acting like a little kid,

or

I'm not going anywhere, you need to go,

or

I can say anything I want, what are you going to do about it?

He could just picture Darrell's smirking face. He was so tired of it.

Alexander had made himself so anxious he couldn't lie still anymore. He got up from bed and paced his bedroom.

He considered taking an extra day off from school so that he could figure things out more. He was fairly confident he could convince Mom and Dad he was a little under the weather. If he could miss a day of school, maybe he could work out a better strategy.

By the morning, though, he was so tired he forgot about the whole idea until he was already face to face with Anthony on the sidewalk.

"Did you think about it?"

"No," he lied.

Anthony glanced at Alexander's feet but didn't say anything about his missing boots.

Not surprisingly, only Vladimir was waiting outside the school when Alexander and Anthony approached the gate.

No Darrell.

Figures.

On the way to Garcia's classroom, Alexander still caught a few Commando Monkey looks from random people, but he got the idea they were disappointed that he wasn't wearing his boots.

Darrell was waiting with everyone else outside Garcia's classroom, facing the other way and talking to Edgar.

Ellen walked up to Alexander. "No boots?"

Alexander looked awkwardly at his feet. "They hurt." *And they're stupid.*

Ellen nodded as if she approved, while Edgar turned at the sound of Alexander's voice.

Darrell turned his wheelchair around.

"Hey." Alexander was almost startled and wanted to make sure he said something *first*.

"Hey," Darrell responded but didn't say anything more.

Alexander had no idea what he should do.

Did Darrell just say *hey* to mock him? It was possible, he decided. *Hey* could mean a lot of things.

Darrell had said *hey* quickly, he thought, almost on top of his own *hey*.

Was he trying to intimidate Alexander with an extra-aggressive *hey?*

What should he do then? Respond with another *hey?* A louder one, maybe? Maybe Darrell was trying to trick him into saying something more than *hey*. Alexander was determined not to let that happen. He'd take the high road. If Darrell wanted trouble, Alexander wasn't going to give it to him.

Anthony poked him in the side, painfully this time, and Alexander refocused on Darrell, who glared at him for a few seconds before asking, "Well?"

Well what?

Alexander realized he'd tranced out so hard on what Darrell might say, he'd missed what he did say. He studied Darrell's expression for some hint. He had a response prepared for every possibility, but he couldn't tell if Darrell was angry or suspicious—he just kept glaring.

Alexander glared back. If what Darrell said was important enough, he figured, he would say it again.

He waited.

Darrell waited.

Then the bell rang.

Ellen watched Darrell turn and head into the classroom, then looked at Alexander. Alexander could tell she was trying to figure out what was going on, but he just shrugged as if he were clueless.

In Garcia's class, Alexander sat toward the back of the room. Anthony was just ahead of him, and Darrell's wheelchair was in the front row. Alexander leaned forward and whispered over Anthony's shoulder, "What did he ask?"

Anthony waved him off. Garcia was already scanning the room to make sure he was the center of attention.

"Can anyone," Garcia began, "define *morality* for the class?"

Alexander knew to avert his eyes when Garcia asked a question. Everyone knew the *Garcia Trick*—keep your eyes on Garcia all the time, but look away when he asked a question. Eye contact was as good as raising a hand. He looked down at his notebook and pretended to take notes.

Thankfully, Garcia called on Joleen, the maddeningly frustrating girl in the back of the room that thought she knew everything—and actually did. She'd answer the question perfectly, slowly, and in detail—and take the pressure off of the rest of them for at least ten minutes.

"Morality is, I think, difficult to define," she began. "If you want to define the word itself, that is a simple definition. If you want to define what is moral and what isn't, then the task is more difficult."

Alexander looked at the back of Darrell's head.

Well, he'd said.

That didn't tell him anything more than *hey*. Darrell also said it with clear hostility—Alexander was sure of that.

Joleen paused, took a deep breath, and continued her explanation. Then she and Garcia launched into a debate, as Alexander expected.

Carefully, Alexander ripped off a corner of notebook paper, wrote, *What did Darrell ask?* and reached up to pass it to Anthony.

Without missing a beat, Garcia swept by and grabbed the note out of Alexander's hand in mid-pass, just as Anthony was about to grab it.

"What did Darrell ask?" Garcia read to the class, abruptly cutting off Joleen.

Alexander expected Garcia to look directly at him, but his gaze was everywhere else.

Darrell turned back to Garcia, confused, and then saw the note in his hand. He glanced at Alexander for only an instant.

He looked annoyed.

"Anyone?" Garcia asked. "What did Darrell ask?"

No one responded.

He looked at Anthony. "Do you know?"

Anthony held his hands out innocently as if he had no idea what was going on.

Garcia abruptly turned around.

"Darrell!"

Darrell looked up at Garcia.

Garcia leaned over his desk. "What did you ask?"

At first, Darrell stared down Garcia just like he did Alexander.

"Nothing important," Darrell answered flatly.

Garcia prodded him. "If it's important enough for *Alexander* to pass a note in class, it's got to be good."

Almost everyone laughed.

Darrell wasn't laughing, though.

Neither was Alexander.

Garcia retreated from Darrell's desk, faked a return to the front of the class, then turned and leaned toward Alexander's face. "I guess you're going to have to wait."

Alexander didn't dare say anything.

Garcia moved closer, getting right in his face and activating the Garcia Stare.

"Until *after* class."

Garcia remained in his face for a full ten seconds—Alexander counted—before finally returning to the front of the classroom. He leaned back on his desk and nodded at Joleen to continue.

For a moment, while Garcia wasn't looking, Darrell glared at Alexander.

Alexander glared back.

Like a lion that wasn't going to back down.

Chapter Eighteen

You Guys are Exactly the Same

As soon as class was over, Alexander positioned himself just outside the door, so Darrell would see him.

Anthony saw him first. "What are you doing?"

"I want to know what he said."

"I didn't say *anything*." Darrell rolled through the doorway and faced him.

"Why did you say *well?*"

"Why wouldn't I?"

Alexander was jostled by someone walking by, but he didn't let it distract him.

"You said *well* like you were waiting for an answer!"

"To what?" Darrell was nearly shouting.

People were starting to gather around as if there would be a fight.

Alexander thought he should shout, too. "You tell me." He had no intention of backing down.

"*GET OUT OF MY DOORWAY!*" Garcia bellowed at a record volume, cutting through the hallway chatter and even leaving an aftermath of startled silence, if only for an instant.

Still, Alexander was going to hold his ground and blame Darrell, but both Anthony and Ellen half-pushed, half-pulled him out of the hallway and outside the building.

It was only then that he realized that they were *laughing*.

"Why are you laughing at me?" Alexander demanded, louder than he'd intended.

Anthony patted him on the shoulder. "We're not laughing at *you*, Alexander."

Alexander imagined the rest of the sentence—they were laughing *with* him.

But that wasn't what they meant at all.

"We're laughing at *both* of you," Ellen clarified.

"*What?*" Darrell was there, though Alexander wasn't sure if he'd come out on his own, or he'd been herded, too.

"You guys are *exactly* the same."

Darrell reddened. "Don't compare me to *him!*"

"Yeah!" For once, Alexander agreed totally with Darrell. At least they had that much in common. Everyone was looking at him—and Darrell—with obnoxious grins.

Frustrated, Alexander threw up his hands, said, "I'm going to P.E.," and slipped into the crowd.

"So am I!"

But they hurried off in different directions.

Alexander didn't look back, but even through the hallway noise, he could swear he heard laughter.

Vladimir still had his stupid smile when he joined Alexander in line at the beginning of P.E.

"I'm nothing like him," Alexander insisted.

"Okay."

"I don't know why you guys think that."

"Okay."

Vladimir was purposely being difficult. Alexander decided not to talk to him again for the rest of class.

They were still playing softball, unfortunately. Alexander had hoped that his two-day absence would get him out of pitching, but he was right back on the mound. On his first pitch, Alexander hit a kid in the shoulder, sending him walking to first base. The kid glared at Alexander as if he'd *meant* to hit him.

When he caught Vladimir looking at him from his shortstop position, he couldn't resist asking again, "How am I like him?"

Vladimir was only barely holding back an all-out laugh. "You both worry too much, first of all."

"Focus on the game!" Ben shouted from first base.

Half an inning later, just before Alexander took his turn at bat, Vladimir nudged him.

"And you both have a temper."

Alexander very nearly proved Vladimir right but tried to stay calm, stomping out to home plate and trying to ignore him.

He concentrated on the pitcher, a boy he vaguely remembered from fourth grade who had a habit of stealing his pens. Alexander still didn't trust him.

Pen-stealer wound up for his pitch.

Alexander checked his stance and gripped the bat as tightly as he possibly could.

He actually hit the ball.

Hard.

It wasn't a home run or anything, but it was enough to get him to first base, which was one base further than he had any dream of reaching.

Vladimir was next at-bat—and he hit the ball, too. Alexander found himself on second base—an entirely new experience. He thought Vladimir was watching him, but he refused to look in his direction.

Then Charlie was at bat and hit an easy home run. Alexander, for the first time he could remember, found himself running for home base.

Just before Ben and Charlie sprinted back to the locker room at the end of class, Ben tapped Alexander on the shoulder. Alexander looked over, and Ben just nodded. Charlie gave him a half-nod, and they both ran off.

He wasn't sure what that was supposed to mean, but he guessed it had something to do with the fact that he'd actually hit the ball and scored a run.

"Hey!" Vladimir called out. He jogged up to Alexander, obviously happy about the game.

"I'm nothing like Darrell," Alexander reminded him, just in case he was going to say anything.

"*And*," Vladimir continued anyway, "you never *let go of anything.*"

Alexander shook his head in frustration and ran ahead of Vladimir for the locker room.

"And you're both grumpy," Vladimir shouted after him. After a few seconds, he added, "Good game."

"Thanks," Alexander grumbled, realizing that he did, in fact, sound grumpy.

Chapter Nineteen

The Prisoner

Colin was gone.

Alexander blinked, just to make sure he wasn't hallucinating. All semester, Colin had been sitting at exactly the same table in the library every single day. Now, as if he'd vanished into thin air, he was gone.

Mr. Lee, meanwhile, was busy behind the front desk, quietly concentrating on his computer screen.

"Hey."

Startled, Alexander turned around.

Darrell had followed him to the library.

"Hey."

Darrell stared at Alexander's bootless feet for a second.

Alexander braced himself for another insult.

"I'm sorry I went overboard with the comments."

At first, Alexander wasn't sure what he should say. Darrell looked up for a response.

"I'm sorry I overreacted," Alexander offered. Their conversation wasn't going anything like he'd imagined.

"Boys?"

Mr. Lee had noticed them hesitating in the doorway.

Alexander turned back and decided to seize the opportunity. He stepped through the door, approached Mr. Lee, and shook his hand, careful to project as bright a smile as he had offered the cops at the hotel in Santa Monica.

"Hi, Mr. Lee!" Alexander tried to sound confident, though he felt horribly uneasy.

Mr. Lee shook his hand. "Hello, Alexander!"

Alexander finally spotted Colin. He was almost hidden now, in a glass-enclosed meeting room behind Mr. Lee's desk. He sat at a large conference table, his books spread before him.

Alexander nodded toward the glass room. "How's Colin?"

Mr. Lee finally pulled away his hand. "He's doing well."

"Can I see him?"

Mr. Lee stepped directly in front of Alexander, purposely blocking his view of Colin. "I'm afraid not."

Darrell pulled up next to Alexander, demanding, "Why?"

"I think you boys need to get to lunch."

"Why can't we see him?" Alexander tried to sound determined, though with Darrell coming to his defense, he was a little confused. He wasn't used to having an ally.

Mr. Lee wouldn't answer. He pointed at the door. "You're going to have to go now."

Alexander managed one more glance at Colin, and then they were standing in the middle of the hallway.

"What's that about?" Darrell asked.

Alexander moved closer to Darrell's wheelchair. He didn't know what to say, much less what to think.

Why did Darrell help me?
Why is Darrell even here?
What happened to Colin?
Why can't I speak to him?
Did Colin do something?
Did I do something?

Alexander had tranced out again. Darrell was already halfway down the hall, heading to lunch. Alexander ran after him. He was almost breathless when he caught up, just as they reached the lunch table.

"Sorry," he told Darrell right away.

Darrell didn't seem concerned, though.

Alexander had thought the group would be surprised to see the two of them together, but everyone looked up at them as if nothing had happened. It could have been any other day.

Ellen seemed more puzzled than anything, studying Darrell, and then Alexander. "What's wrong?"

Alexander sat down, unsure of what he should say. "Do you guys know that kid that's always in the library?"

Vladimir nodded. "Library Boy!"

"Colin," Alexander corrected.

"What about him?" Ellen asked.

Alexander hesitated.

"He's like a prisoner," Darrell suggested.

"Yeah," Alexander said. "Mr. Lee won't even let me talk to him."

"I know Colin!" Edgar announced. "He's a transfer. From Wickshire."

Wickshire was the next middle school over.

"I was supposed to take him around and show him the campus," Edgar explained, then admitted sheepishly, "but then they didn't want me to do it anymore."

Darrell turned to Alexander. "He wouldn't have to know the rest of the school if he never leaves the library."

"Maybe he's just antisocial," Vladimir suggested.

"He's not, though." Alexander had thought that Colin was actually pretty friendly. "Do you know *why* he transferred?" he asked Edgar.

Edgar shook his head.

"Maybe he got expelled," Darrell suggested.

Alexander shook his head. "No. It's something else." Colin just didn't seem like *that* kind of kid.

Everyone at the table was quiet, waiting for Alexander to continue. He realized they were listening—really concentrating—on what he had to say. It scared him to the point that he nearly forgot what he was talking about. He stared down at the table, took a deep breath, and tried to calm himself down. This was way too important to mess up.

"They won't let him make friends," he said, uncertain if he was making any sense at all.

He looked up again.

"But why?" Ellen asked.

Alexander didn't know the answer.

"I've *got* to talk to him," he concluded.

"But you said he's locked down," Vladimir pointed out.

"I think I have a plan—" he nearly chickened out before he continued, but decided to push ahead and say it, "—if you guys help."

No one responded at first.

Darrell slapped the armrest of his wheelchair.

Alexander was startled at first, but Darrell broke out into a broad smile.

"You know we will."

Chapter Twenty

Alexander's Pride

You know we will.

As soon as Darrell had uttered those words, Alexander realized he *shouldn't* have been surprised, even though he was. He knew his friends would come through, even though he was afraid they wouldn't. He couldn't imagine why he didn't get it until now.

He didn't need to care about the trolls, or being called weird, odd, or Commando Monkey. His friends were behind him, so he *owned* the trolls and everything they said.

Even if they called him scrawny.

Alexander took a deep breath. He remembered his dad up on stage, talking to hundreds of people at once with amazing ease.

"When a pride of lions hunt," he made sure to make eye contact with everyone, "they don't all just run after their prey. They work together and drive him into their trap."

"We're going to hunt Colin?" Anthony asked, sounding almost horrified.

"I'm talking about Mr. Lee."

"We're hunting Mr. Lee?" Edgar's voice cracked.

"No," Alexander patiently answered, "but we are going to lure him into a trap."

Darrell slapped the armrest of his wheelchair again. For an instant, Alexander was unnerved. Usually, that was Darrell's sign of frustration with him. One look, though, and Alexander realized that Darrell was excited.

Everyone was paying attention, and everyone liked what he was saying. For the first time, he realized how Dad felt.

Step by step, he explained his plan. It was difficult without his phone, but he had it all planned out in his head. At the end of the day, they had ten minutes to act after the final bell rang and before Mr. Lee walked Colin out to the red truck. They would have to move quickly.

Alexander made assignments and synchronized everyone's watches.

At 2:56 p.m., school was over.

At 2:58 p.m., they met outside the library.

Alexander stepped in first and surveyed the situation, pretending to browse through the magazine rack.

Colin was in his "glass cage."

Mr. Lee was at the counter, checking out a book for a girl Alexander recognized from history class.

As planned, the others entered in ones or twos, so they wouldn't call attention to themselves, and took up their assigned positions.

Anthony came in first and casually browsed the science books near the big windows on the far side of the library.

Vladimir came in next and pretended to browse the science fiction aisle.

Darrell went over to check out the catalog at one of the computer stations near the front counter, while Edgar took another computer right next to his.

Michael and Josh, another kid from the Art Club, walked in. They took over tables directly between Colin and Mr. Lee.

Finally, Ellen walked in and took up her position at the far end of the second aisle, browsing in the astronomy section.

Everyone was in place. Mr. Lee hadn't noticed a thing.

Alexander nodded at Darrell, who turned in his wheelchair to face Mr. Lee.

"I have to write a report on child soldiers in the Civil War. Can you help me?"

Mr. Lee smiled kindly and led Darrell, as Alexander had planned, to the stacks below the big windows on the other side of the library.

Perfect.

When a pride of lions hunted, Alexander knew, they worked as a team. Just like any team, they all had specific roles. The Wings circled the prey and guided it to the Center, who would then go for the kill.

As Mr. Lee guided Darrell down the center aisle toward the Civil War stacks, Anthony moved from the science books to meet them, saying hi to Darrell and asking Mr. Lee to help him, too, when he was finished with Darrell. He stood by, crowding them ever so slightly.

Vladimir emerged from around the other aisle holding a science fiction book and asked Mr. Lee about his opinion.

Mr. Lee was all smiles with so many active readers and joyfully held up his hands. "You'll just have to wait your turn!"

The group finally reached the Civil War stacks, where Ellen had squarely placed herself.

"I beg your pardon," Mr. Lee said, and everyone laughed. Ellen laughed and apologized, asked Darrell what he was looking for, and carried on a nonstop stream of conversation. Mr. Lee just kept grinning. He had no idea he'd been sent right into the jaws of the Center, and Ellen was ready to pounce. She kept talking, and the boys stood by Mr. Lee, forming a solid wall between him and front of the library.

Michael stood over Josh as if to tutor him on some fine point—and further block any view of Colin.

Edgar took up a position by a paperback rack just outside the glass room, completing the human wall obscuring Mr. Lee's view.

For an instant, Alexander wondered if the door to the conference room would be locked, and was relieved to find it open. He walked into the small room and sat opposite Colin.

"Hey," Alexander said.

Colin looked up after a moment and looked through the window at the library.

"Usually, the *Wings* are girls."

"Yeah," Alexander agreed, "but the *Center's* a girl, and she's already gone in for the kill."

Alexander thought he might have seen a hint of a smile, but Colin looked off again as if he were trying to spot Mr. Lee.

"He wouldn't let me talk to you," Alexander said.

Colin's smile disappeared and he looked down.

"How come?" Alexander asked.

At almost a whisper, Colin admitted, "I didn't do too well at my last school."

"Did you get expelled?"

Colin just shook his head. Alexander could almost feel him slipping back into his books.

A hundred possibilities flew through his head. Colin wasn't—how else could he think of it?—normal-looking. The pale skin, thin, almost skeletal build, and his shaky voice made him unlike anyone Alexander had ever known. Was Colin sick? Infected?

Don't think like that.

There was something different, though—something Alexander had only just seen.

What was it?

Colin looked the same. He was still dressed in all black, wearing the same turtleneck sweater. He hadn't much changed since the first time Alexander had noticed Library Boy.

Colin gazed at the lion encyclopedia, open again in front of him. "I was like prey—"

"—in a sea of predators?"

Colin nodded.

"That's why you left your old school?"

"Lions never go after the strongest buffalo," Colin explained. "They go after the slow one, the one that can't keep up, the straggler."

"You're not a buffalo."

"I'm not a lion, either." Colin's shaky voice seemed almost strangled now as if he could barely talk.

Alexander looked toward the back of the library. Darrell, Anthony, and Vladimir were still running interference, and Ellen was still talking—monopolizing Mr. Lee's attention. He turned back to Colin.

"Well, neither am I."

Somehow, that made Colin smile again, and Alexander added, "I just make the most of what I've got."

That moment, Alexander realized what had changed about Colin.

Colin was actually looking at him. He wasn't looking down, or looking away, or talking to the air.

Alexander gazed through the conference room window at Edgar, who was watching him from the paperback rack, waiting for his signal. He turned back to Colin.

"This isn't right."

Colin looked down at the tabletop again.

"You're like a prisoner."

"I'm not a prisoner." Colin stared at his closed notebook as if he could see through to the pages inside.

"They can't force you to stay here."

For a moment, Colin was silent. Then he looked up.

"They didn't force me," he admitted quietly.

If they didn't force Colin to stay in the library, Alexander realized, there really was only one other reason.

It was his choice.

When Alexander didn't respond right away, Colin whispered, "I told you I'm not a lion."

Alexander nodded down at Colin's copy of *A Complete Encyclopedia of Lions*. "You know, there's one big difference between humans and lions."

Colin considered the book, too, but he was stumped. "What?"

Alexander nodded at Edgar. He, Michael, and Josh moved closer to the library entrance.

Colin watched them curiously.

Alexander scanned the library one more time, then told Colin, "I didn't come all the way out here to the Serengeti to come back empty-handed."

Alexander stood up.

Colin hesitated, unsure of what he should do.

"Come on," Alexander encouraged him.

"But what's the difference?"

Alexander reached under the table, grabbed Colin's backpack—it was really more of a briefcase—and dropped it on the table.

"Come on."

Colin stared at his backpack so long that Alexander thought he might not move at all. Finally, he pulled his books together and packed away his things. He stood up.

"Okay."

Alexander led the way out of the conference room and out of the library.

In the deserted hallway, Alexander paused a moment, looked up at Colin, and explained, "We can be a lion if we want to be."

Colin gazed back at the door to the library.

"Come on," Alexander said.

As soon as Colin turned back to him, Alexander took a couple of steps down the hall, hesitating just long enough to see that Colin was following.

In a moment, Colin caught up, and together they exited school through the north gate.

Alexander led Colin as far as the sidewalk. They stopped, turned around, and watched the gate until, one by one, their friends appeared, crossed the sidewalk, and rejoined the pride.

READ THE ENTIRE SERIES!

...and check out RichPerceptions.com to discover more from Rich Samuels!

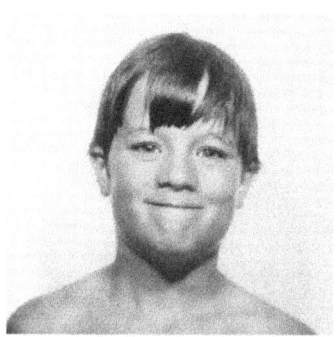

RiCH SAMUELS realized he was a writer when
he was nine years old. Even though
he's an Emmy™-winning video producer, he considers himself
a writer first. *Alexander Adventures* and his other novels
are made for kids who like books with good laughs and real kids.
One young reader wrote of Rich's books:

"...you feel as though you're best friends with the characters."

To find out more about the author, visit
RichPerceptions.com

www.ingramcontent.com/pod-product-compliance
Lightning Source LLC
Chambersburg PA
CBHW071514040426
42444CB00008B/1639